16 Developmental Tests
For
Managers & Supervisors

by

Louis E. Tagliaferri, Ph.D.

Ponte Vedra, Florida 32082
904-285-7757
www.talico.com

Published by Louis E. Tagliaferri
Ponte Vedra Beach, Florida 32082
Printed in the United States of America

ISBN-13: 978-1496149558
ISBN-10: 1496149556

Dedicated to the thousands of managers,
supervisors and candidates for those positions
in business, industry and government who have
benefited from the developmental attributes of
the assessments and tests in this compendium.

Table of Contents

Introduction

This is a compendium of developmental instruments designed to help HRD and Training Professionals and other Executives assess the interaction skills of managers, supervisors and candidates for those positions. It is stressed that none of the instruments in this series is designed to determine the suitability of any employee for selection for employment, for promotion or for advancement or for the suitability of the position that the employee may currently hold. Instead, their purpose is to help HRD and Training Professionals and other Executives understand the training and development needs of employees.

The instruments in this compendium can be used singly or as part of a series. For example, a facilitator might choose to administer only the Supervisory Skills Test to a group of current or prospective supervisors, team leaders or lead persons in order to obtain diagnostic information that will help the facilitator design a supervisory training course. Alternatively, The Supervisory Skills Test can be paired with a leadership instrument such as the Leadership Skills Test in order to obtain a broader diagnostic perspective. Similarly, the five team assessments can be used either singly or in combination in a structured team building training course.

Each instrument consists of an Administration Manual or Facilitator's Guide and a Participant's Booklet. The former includes a synopsis of the instrument and facilitation guidelines and scoring information. The Participant's Booklet is essentially a "test booklet." Purchase of this book includes a limited license for the purchaser to reproduce and use any or all of the material contained herein for educational and developmental purposes. Refer to the Reproduction Notice for additional information regarding reproducibility.

It is strongly recommended that facilitators thoroughly familiarize themselves with the principles upon which the instruments are based before administering them to employees. Such preparation will enhance participant confidence in the results of the assessments and avoid a situation where a participant might challenge a "correct" answer and the facilitator is unable to explain the answer rationale satisfactorily.

Communication
Effectiveness Scale

by
Louis E. Tagliaferri, Ph.D.

Administration Guide
MD-101

TITLE: COMMUNICATION EFFECTIVENESS SCALE

PURPOSE: To evaluate the quality of communication practices among managers and supervisors. To provide feedback and to facilitate coaching with respect to perceived communication effectiveness.

DESCRIPTION: This scale measures perceptions about communication practice effectiveness in six key communication skill dimensions. Categories covered include verbal communication, written communication, listening skills, coaching & counseling, intergroup (with peers and superiors) communication and performance communication. Six sets of eight items each comprise the forty-eight total items in the instrument. Respondents are asked to assess the communication practices of the person being rated by indicating their perception in each item on a Likert type scale. Multi-level format facilitates ratings by three organizational levels. Scores are calculated per category and for total communication effectiveness.

VALIDITY: the construct, or syndrome of interrelated behaviors, which is covered by this instrument is both important and useful. In the design of the instrument every reasonable effort was made to ensure proper universe of content, simplicity of item wording and minimization of acquiescence and social desirability.

ADMINISTRATION: Self or facilitator administered. Multi-level (superior, self, peer or subordinate) measurement option. Requires 20-25 minutes.

APPLICATION: Communication Skills Development
                    Organization Improvement
                    Human Relations Training
                    Self/Professional/Career Development
                    Coaching & Counseling
                    Performance Improvement

SUITABLE FOR: Line & Staff Managers
                    Superiors
                    Non-Supervisory "management" level employees
                    Employees at other levels on a selected basis

SCORING: See scoring format following.

HOW THE CES CAN BE USED

The Communication Effectiveness Scale (CES) is a highly versatile instrument that has many possible applications. The instrument is designed to measure perceptions about the communication skills effectiveness of managers and supervisors. It can also be used for non-managers and supervisors by simply disregarding those few items that directly relate to communication interaction with subordinates. The CES is designed in multi-level format in order to obtain assessment perceptions not only from an individual respondent but also from his/her superior, subordinates and/or peers.

Most organizations use the CES for developmental purposes. In this way CES assessments are obtained for individuals and are then used for coaching and counseling sessions or as part of an experiential learning process in a communication skills training course. The CES is also an excellent diagnostic instrument that can be used as the basis for an organization development effort aimed toward improving overall organizational communication effectiveness.

HOW TO ADMINISTER THE CES

In order to obtain optimum value from the CES we recommend that you administer it not only to the person whose communication skills are being assessed but also to his/her superior, subordinates and/or peers. One copy of the CES is required for each person who will be completing it for a subject person. A total of 5-7 subordinates (or peers) for each subject person will usually be sufficient to provide an accurate rating from that organizational level. Be sure that subordinates or peers are randomly selected. Also, be sure to average the ratings of subordinates or peers. It is important that subordinate/peer level responses be anonymous (except for identification of the organizational level they represent).

The CES can be administered to employees in group or to them singly. Proctored administration is recommended but not required. Allow 20-25 minutes for completion.

Scoring information will be found on the last page of this guide.

HOW TO SCORE IT

The CES can easily be scored by following these steps:

1. Point Values for response alternatives are: Strongly Agree = 4, Somewhat Agree = 3, Somewhat Disagree = 2, Strongly Disagree = 1.

2. Plot the individual item ratings of the manager or supervisor (SELF) and his or her SUPERIOR in each grid as appropriate. Identify the different ratings with symbols such as * = SELF, X = SUPERIOR.

3. Average the SUBORDINATES/PEERS' scores for each CES item and plot the averages in each set grid as above: O = SUB/PEERS.

4. Total the CES item scores for each level within the space to the right of each grid.

5. Total the SELF, SUPERIOR, and SUB/PEERS' scores to arrive at a set score.

6. Set scores below 64 and individual CES ITEM scores (the total of all three levels) below 9 indicate that the manager or supervisor would likely benefit from additional communication skill development.

7. Be sure to carefully study the individual item ratings to identify any significant perceptual differences among the rating levels. Significant perceptual differences could indicate other problems such as poor communication, unclear role/responsibility definition, etc.

EXAMPLE

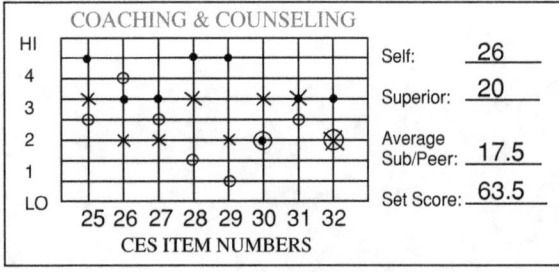

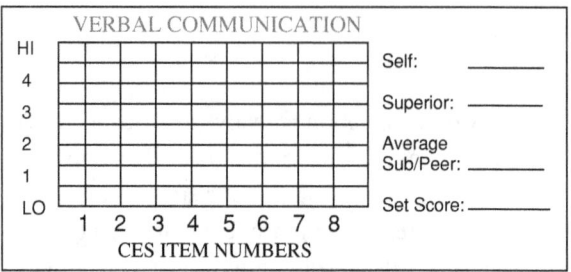

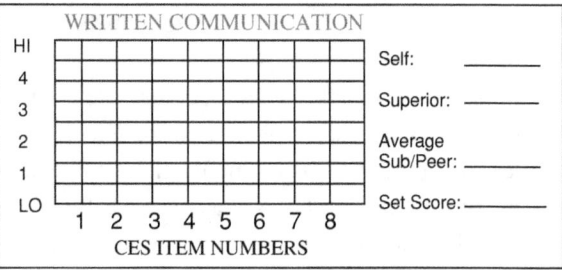

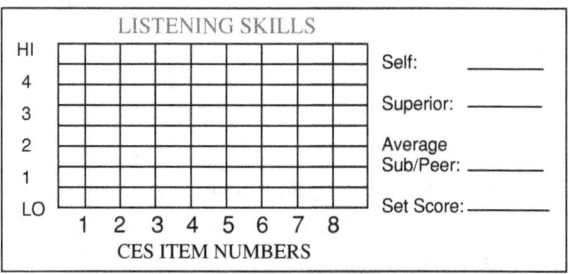

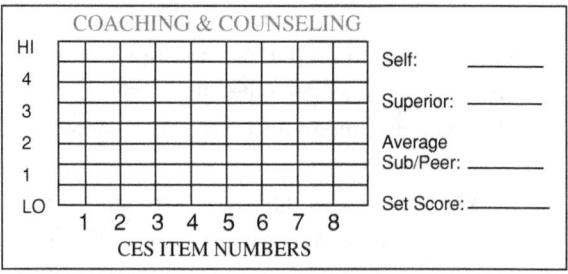

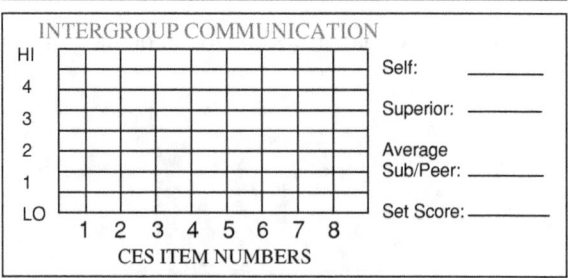

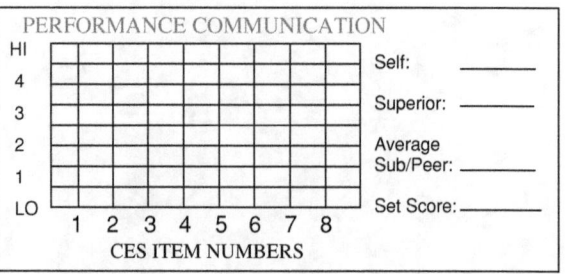

Communication Effectiveness Scale

by
Louis E. Tagliaferri, Ph.D.

Participant Booklet
MD-101

Organization:
Name:
You Are:
☐   The Above Person
☐   A Subordinate/Peer of the Above Person
☐   The Superior of the Above Person

Instructions: This questionnire describes 48 practices that commonly occur when managers and supervisors communicate with others. Decide the extent to which each practice is characterstic of the person being rated (whose name appears on the front cover of this questionnaire). Then indicate your decision by placing a check mark in the appropriate column to the right of each practice.

WHEN COMMUNICATING VERBALLY THE PERSON BEING RATED:

		Strongly Agree	Somewhat Agree	Somewhat Disagree	Strongly Disagree
1.	Chooses words with care.	❐	❐	❐	❐
2.	Defines key terms clearly.	❐	❐	❐	❐
3.	Commands the necessary vocabulary.	❐	❐	❐	❐
4.	Expresses thoughts clearly.	❐	❐	❐	❐
5.	Avoids ambiguity.	❐	❐	❐	❐
6.	Uses good voice tone and variety.	❐	❐	❐	❐
7.	Speaks in a clear, articulate manner.	❐	❐	❐	❐
8.	Minimizes the use of jargon, slang or code terms.	❐	❐	❐	❐

WHEN COMMUNICATING IN WRITING THE PERSON BEING RATED:

9.	Uses a natural, appropriate writing style.	❐	❐	❐	❐
10.	Avoids vagueness and generalities.	❐	❐	❐	❐
11.	Keeps sentences and paragraphs short.	❐	❐	❐	❐
12.	Uses proper grammar, spelling and punctuation.	❐	❐	❐	❐
13.	Organizes message in a logical way.	❐	❐	❐	❐
14.	Includes all the material necessary to convey the message.	❐	❐	❐	❐
15.	Keeps messages concise and simple.	❐	❐	❐	❐
16.	Uses examples or illustrations to help convey the message.	❐	❐	❐	❐

WHEN LISTENING TO OTHERS THE PERSON BEING RATED:

17.	Concentrates on what is being said.	❐	❐	❐	❐
18.	Defers judgement or evaluation.	❐	❐	❐	❐
19.	Avoids interrupting the speaker.	❐	❐	❐	❐
20.	Keeps an open mind.	❐	❐	❐	❐
21.	Listens for ideas rather than for words.	❐	❐	❐	❐
22.	Listens without prejudice or bias.	❐	❐	❐	❐
23.	Encourages others to speak and to build information.	❐	❐	❐	❐
24.	Provides feedback to acknowledge receipt of the message.	❐	❐	❐	❐

WHEN COACHING AND COUNSELING SUBORDINATES THE PERSON BEING RATED:

25.	Is friendly and approachable.	❏	❏	❏	❏
26.	Tries to understand the basis of employees' concerns.	❏	❏	❏	❏
27.	Shows fairness and impartiality.	❏	❏	❏	❏
28.	Respects what is said in confidence.	❏	❏	❏	❏
29.	Uses effective interviewing techniques.	❏	❏	❏	❏
30.	Remains calm in emotional situations.	❏	❏	❏	❏
31.	Encourages upward communication from subordinates.	❏	❏	❏	❏
32.	Facilitates rather than dominates.	❏	❏	❏	❏

WHEN COMMUNICATING WITH PEERS AND SUPERIORS THE PERSON BEING RATED:

33.	Avoids oversimplifying complex issues.	❏	❏	❏	❏
34.	Offers opinions and suggestions candidly.	❏	❏	❏	❏
35.	Discusses controversial issues openly and honestly.	❏	❏	❏	❏
36.	Has the ability to empathize with others.	❏	❏	❏	❏
37.	Resolves conflict through problem solving.	❏	❏	❏	❏
38.	Presents recommendations persuasively.	❏	❏	❏	❏
39.	Maintains friendly, harmonious relationships.	❏	❏	❏	❏
40.	Accepts constructive criticism maturely.	❏	❏	❏	❏

WHEN COMMUNICATING WITH SUBORDINATES ABOUT JOB PERFORMANCE THE PERSON BEING RATED:

41.	Gives clear, understandable instructions.	❏	❏	❏	❏
42.	Obtains feedback to ensure that instructions are understood.	❏	❏	❏	❏
43.	Establishes clear, measurable and realistic work standards.	❏	❏	❏	❏
44.	Informs employees about what is expected of them.	❏	❏	❏	❏
45.	Provides constructive performance feedback.	❏	❏	❏	❏
46.	Provides sufficient job related information.	❏	❏	❏	❏
47.	Encourages suggestions for improvement.	❏	❏	❏	❏
48.	Controls the "grapevine."	❏	❏	❏	❏

Intercultural
Communication Inventory

By
Louis E. Tagliaferri, Ph.D.

Administration Guide
TB-407ELG

How to Use it

The Intercultural Communication Inventory (ICI) is most effective when used as a training aid to increase knowledge and awareness about intercultural communication concepts and principles. It can serve equally well as an excellent "ice breaker" or as a closure exercise. Although designed primarily as a learning instrument, the ICI can also be used to help evaluate the effectiveness of a diversity or intercultural relations workshop or seminar by being administered as a "post-test." Still another use is to help stimulate intercultural communication discussion among continuous improvement teams, self-directed work teams and other work unit teams.

In order to obtain optimum value from the ICI, facilitators should first read both this guide and the instrument in its entirety. Facilitators should have (or acquire) a fundamental understanding about diversity management and intercultural communication before they use the ICI or conduct an intercultural communication training session. Many good references are readily available if it is necessary to review the subject further.

One copy of the Respondent Booklet is required for each person in the class, team or workshop. Distribute the booklets to all participants. Explain your purpose for administering the instrument and then read the instructions aloud. Allow about 15 minutes for completion. When all participants are finished, ask them to refer to their copy of the inventory. Provide them with the correct answer and conduct a brief discussion about each point covered. Use the intercultural communication tips in the following section of this guide and/or other supplemental material as the basis for this discussion.

Answers & Intercultural Communication Tips

01.   True. Women, minorities and people from other countries who come from different cultural backgrounds are the most rapidly growing sector of the work force.

02.   True. This is "cultural shock." Cultural shock is an intercultural dysfunction that can affect people of all cultures. It also can cause serious identity problems.

03.   False. In fact, this is one of the major reasons why communication between and among people of different cultures often becomes distorted. Misunderstandings occur when people of one culture, including racial, ethnic and religious minorities, interpret the verbal and non-verbal behavior of people of other cultures on the basis of their own values, customs and codes.

04.   False. There is often very little correlation between a person's accent and their comprehension and ease of use of the English language.

05.   False. Human needs and traits may be the same or similar but there are often many significant differences in gestures and expressions. The ringed fingers "OK" symbol, for example, means that everything is "OK" in some cultures but is an obscene gesture in others.

06. False. A good example can be found by studying ancient cultures like the Mayan. Although having a low level of technology as we know it today, the Mayan culture was very advanced and sophisticated in other ways.

07. False. Some cultures place such heavy emphasis on group and team behavior that individuals would be embarrassed if their personal achievements were singled out.

08. True. Although sometimes misleading, first impressions often provide valuable information about a person's profession, economic status, age, personality and other characteristics.

09. True. Further, most people unconsciously become quite proficient at reading the body language of others. The problem is that body language communication is not identical among all cultures.

10. False. The North American communication culture is low context. High context cultures rely heavily on the implied meaning of what is said or not said and how it is said. North Americans are much more explicit and direct.

11. True. See #8 above.

12. True. This can cause the misunderstanding that employees of these cultures do not take the initiative or that they are not motivated.

13. True. Space or distance between speakers has meaning and varies between cultures. In some cultures, it is common for relative strangers to speak in literally face-to-face closeness while, in other cultures, this would be considered too intimate.

14. False. Just the opposite is true; they vary considerably among the cultures of the world.

15. False. In some cultures, smiling and nodding are ways to cover up embarrassment or attempts to please the speaker.

16. False. Many of the world's cultures see time as being much more elastic than the way North Americans see it. For example, the North American focus on adhering to schedules and deadlines is not shared the same way by people in Arab and Latin American countries.

17. True. A common misunderstanding is that it is non-verbal communication.

18. False. All of these factors affect not only interpersonal relationships but also communication. In fact, if not properly understood by communicators they can seriously distort communication between cultures.

19. False. What is most important is for managers and employees of different cultures to develop a better understanding of their respective cultural differences and how these differences can affect relationships and communication.

20. False. Foreign language skills can help. However, cultural awareness and effective intercultural communication, even through interpreters if necessary, is more important.

21. True. Equal Employment Opportunity and Affirmative Action, though both very important, are equity issues. It is possible to have EEO and Affirmative Action programs and still not effectively manage diversity or have effective intercultural communication.

22. False. This may be appropriate when communicating with other low context cultures. However, many cultures within the work place are high context cultures which require less direct, holistic communication.

23. True. Ethnocentrism occurs when cultural groups increasingly focus on their own culture. Communication difficulties increase when two or more ethnocentric groups attempt to communicate with each other. Not sharing common values, etc., they often view the other person as a "stranger" and approach him/her with anxiety and uncertainty.

24. False. Very often they are unaware of the cultural differences and cannot understand why their communication is misinterpreted.

25. True. See #24 above.

Recommended Reading

Cherry, C., World Communication: Threat or Promise? New York, John Wiley & Sons, Inc., 1978.

Harris, Philip R. and Moran, Robert T., Managing Cultural Differences (2nd ed), Houston, Gulf Publishing Company, 1987.

Kim, Young Yun and Gudykunst, William B., Theories in Intercultural Communication, Newbury Park, CA, Sage Publications, 1988.

Samovar, Larry A. and Porter, Richard E., eds., Intercultural Communication: A Reader, Belmont, CA, Wadsworth Publishing, 1972.

Zimpfer, Forest and Underwood, Robert, The Status of International Business Communication Training in the 100 Largest Multinational United States Corporations, Ypsilanti, MI, Eastern Michigan University Report, 1989.

Participant Booklet for

INTERCULTURAL COMMUNICATION INVENTORY

by Louis Tagliaferri, Ph.D.

TB-407

| DATE: |
| ORGANIZATION: |
| WORK GROUP: |
| NAME: |

Instructions: This is a learning instrument which will help you to gain a better understanding about important intercultural communication principles. Read each of the statements below carefully. Decide whether the statement is True (T), False (F) or whether you are Uncertain (?) about it. Then indicate your decision by placing a mark in the appropriate column to the right of each statement.

		T	F	?
01.	Experts predict that by the turn of the century about 80% of the American work force will be made up of women, minorities, and persons from other countries.	☐	☐	☐
02.	Failure or inability of members of one culture to understand members of another often results in problems like anxiety, disorientation, depression, and sleep disorders.	☐	☐	☐
03.	In order to improve communication among different cultures, it is helpful to first interpret other cultural situations according to the values of one's own culture.	☐	☐	☐
04.	As a general rule, a strong foreign accent indicates that the speaker does not have a good understanding of English grammar and vocabulary.	☐	☐	☐
05.	Because people of all cultures share common human traits, non-verbal communication like gestures and facial expressions mean the same thing all over the world.	☐	☐	☐
06.	It is now widely accepted that a low level of technological sophistication indicates an inherently inferior culture.	☐	☐	☐
07.	Recognizing and praising the achievements of an individual is one management practice that is universally accepted among all cultures.	☐	☐	☐
08.	First impressions about people are often quite accurate.	☐	☐	☐
09.	About 65% of a message's meaning is conveyed through non-verbal behavior.	☐	☐	☐
10.	The communication culture in North America is mostly high context; i.e. much of the meaning and understanding is acquired via the context of the message.	☐	☐	☐
11.	Appearance is an important non-verbal communication attribute because it gives information about a person's age, gender, race, culture, and profession.	☐	☐	☐
12.	Asians, Hispanics and some Europeans may not initiate tasks without specific instructions because they consider that doing so challenges the authority of a supervisory.	☐	☐	☐
13.	A potential barrier to intercultural communication is the physical distance between the speaker and the receiver.	☐	☐	☐
14.	Thought patterns, forms of reasoning and logic are universal human behaviors which occur the same way among all cultures.	☐	☐	☐

		T	F	?

15. A smiling, nodding response by an employee to a supervisor's instructions always indicates understanding. ☐ ☐ ☐

16. All cultures tend to view the use of time the same way. ☐ ☐ ☐

17. Sign language that is used by the deaf is considered to be verbal communication. ☐ ☐ ☐

18. Attitudes, the social organization of cultures and roles in society affect relationships among people of different cultures but not communication between them. ☐ ☐ ☐

19. In order to minimize intercultural misunderstandings, managers should emphasize the need for culturally diverse employees to adopt "mainstream" American values and norms. ☐ ☐ ☐

20. Foreign language skills are essential in order to work effectively with people of other cultures. ☐ ☐ ☐

21. Cultural diversity has little to do with Equal Employment and Affirmative Action. ☐ ☐ ☐

22. In order to obtain feedback from an employee of another culture, a manager should always ask precise, direct questions. ☐ ☐ ☐

23. The more groups differ in culture the greater the possibility of communication difficulties between them. ☐ ☐ ☐

24. Intercultural communicators are usually fully aware of the cultural differences that distort communication between them. ☐ ☐ ☐

25. For the most part, intercultural communicators are perceived to be strangers to each other. ☐ ☐ ☐

JOB SKILLS TRAINING NEEDS ASSESSMENT

by Louis E. Tagliaferri, PhD

Facilitator Guide

ORGANIZATION: PROJECT: DATE:

CIRCLE THE JSTNA SECTIONS TO BE COMPLETED

DATA:	0	1	2	3	4	5	6
PEOPLE:	0	1	2	5	6	7	8
THINGS:	0	1	2	4	5	6	7

SYNOPSIS

TITLE: Job Skills Training Needs Assessment (JSTNA)

PURPOSE: The purpose of the JSTNA is to help improve employee job performance by identifying training needs related to the worker functions required for particular occupations.

DESCRIPTION: The Talico Inc. Job Skills Training Needs Assessment is a 105 item instrument that measures up to 21 job skill areas in three primary worker functions categories; the specific functions that employees engage in as they deal with data, people and things (equipment and machines). Facilitators select those sections of the JSTNA that are relevant to each employee's job. A 5-point modified Likert type scale is used to record employees' responses. The instrument has been designed to measure training needs for employees in a broad range of non-supervisory administrative, clerical, sales, customer service, health care and technical-professional capacities and is applicable to most jobs in those groups.

VALIDITY: The design for this instrument is based an extensive study of occupational characteristics, traits and worker job functions for almost 20,000 jobs that were defined, classified and evaluated by the U.S. Department of Labor, Employment and Training Administration.

FACILITATION: Administered and scored by in-house facilitators. Requires from 15 to 30 minutes to complete depending on the number of skill dimensions relevant to a particular job.

APPLICATION: Training needs analysis, career counseling, performance coaching and counseling.

SUITABLE FOR: Non-supervisory employees in commercial, industrial and governmental organizations.

Description

The Job Skills Training Needs Assessment (JSTNA) is a developmental assessment instrument that has been designed to evaluate worker functions training needs among non-supervisory employees in administrative, clerical, sales, customer service, technical-professional and health care related capacities. The concept for the JSTNA is based on job analyses conducted by the U.S. Department of Labor Employment and Training Administration that cover almost 20,000 jobs in all sectors of business, industry and government. The system used to classify and evaluate the relative complexity of these positions is published in the *Dictionary of Occupational Titles (DOT) Fourth Edition, Revised 1991, U.S. Government Printing Office.*

The JSTNA embodies the DOT premise that every job requires, to some extent, the ability to function with respect to data, people and things (equipment and machines). A hierarchy has been established in the DOT for each of the three primary worker functions categories. The three categories together with a ranking of the worker functions within each are shown in the following table:

Structure of Worker functions

Data (1st digit)	**People** (2nd digit)	**Things** (3rd digit)
0 Synthesizing	0 Mentoring	0 Setting Up
1 Coordinating	1 Negotiating	1 Precision Working
2 Analyzing	2 Instructing	2 Operating-Controlling
3 Compiling	3 Supervising	3 Driving-Operating
4 Computing	4 Diverting	4 Manipulating
5 Copying	5 Persuading	5 Tending
6 Comparing	6 Speaking-Signaling	6 Feeding-offbearing
	7 Serving	7 Handling
	8 Taking Instructions-Helping	

*Note: The functions of supervising and diverting in the **People** category, and Driving-Operating in the **Things** category are not included in the JSTNA because they are not relevant to the jobs which the JSTNA is designed to assess. The corresponding number of sets for these functions will not be found in the JSTA questionnaire.*

The DOT has classified all jobs according to a nine digit numeric system that arranges jobs by occupational groups and titles and also ranks them according to levels of complexity. In the DOT system, the three middle digits of the nine digit code denote job complexity. The first of the three digits represents **Data**, the second digit represents **People** and the third digit represents **Thing** worker functions. A lower number in a given category indicates more complex responsibility and judgement and a higher number indicates tasks that are, in general, less complicated and that require lower skill levels. For example, in the **Data** category the tasks "Coordinating" and "Analyzing" are more complex tasks than "Computing" or "Copying".

The three digit worker functions code is a way to classify occupations which require an individual to perform tasks that are similar in complexity. This code is not specific to any occupation or industry. It can apply to any number of occupations or jobs that require similar skills, knowledge or responsibility level.

As an example, suppose we have a job classified with worker functions code 257. In the **Data** category, the highest level of expertise or responsibility needed to effectively perform a job with code 257 is "Analyzing". In relation to **People**, "Persuading" is the highest function necessary to effectively perform this job and in relation to **Things**, the task of "Handling" is the only requirement. It is assumed, then, that the individual doing this job can generally perform any task with a higher number than the one given by the worker functions code for a given category. Therefore, an individual in this job should also be able to effectively perform the **Data** tasks of "compiling", "computing", "copying" and "comparing" if required.

The JSTNA has organized a broad range of benchmark jobs into seven common occupational groups. The three digit worker functions code assigned in the DOT is listed to the left of each job title in the **List of Occupational Groups & Titles** (see **Appendix A**). This code indicates the core sections of the JSTNA questionnaire which an employee should complete in order to evaluate his or her training needs. (See **Administering the JSTNA**, paragraph #5 for further details about selecting sections to complete for a particular job.)

The JSTNA is intended to evaluate training needs by assessing the extent to which both an employee and his or her supervisor believe that the employee's job performance will be enhanced by further training in the job functions relevant to the employee's job. In order to accomplish this facilitators are asked to match employees' current job titles as closely as possible with one of the titles listed in the **List of Occupational Groups & Titles**.

It is recognized that titles and responsibilities can vary considerably from job to job and from organization to organization. However, the benchmark jobs in the **List of Occupational Groups & Titles** were carefully selected from among the thousands available as being among the most common and most illustrative of the titled occupations that are found throughout business, industry and government. Because of this, it should be possible to find a reasonably close match between the jobs of most employees in most organizations and the jobs suggested by the titles in the **List of Occupational Groups & Titles**.

How to Administer the JSTNA

The Job Skills Training Needs Assessment is divided in 3 worker functions categories that consist of a total of 21 sections or sets of items. Each section represents a general skill dimension and corresponds with a specific set of related worker functions. Employees are required to complete only those sections of the JSTNA that the facilitator has determined corresponds with their job as designated by the code and description in the **List of Occupational Groups & Titles**.

The following guidelines will help you to successfully administer the test and obtain optimum value from it for all respondents:

1. Before you begin the test, take a few minutes to read all of the material included in this manual.

2. Refer to the **List of Occupational Groups & Titles** in this guide. Read the summary description of each occupational group to help determine which occupational group most closely corresponds with the employees's job classification. For example, if the employee holds the job of a clerk-typist his or her occupational group is **Clerical**. If he or she is a budget analyst then the appropriate occupational group is **Administrative**.

3. Once you locate the employee's occupational group, find the job title that is closest to the type of work that he or she does. For example, if the employee handles customer inquiries or complaints, the job title within the **List of Occupational Groups & Titles** that most closely corresponds with his or her job is probably **Customer Service Representative**.

4. The **List of Occupational Groups & Titles** contains benchmark occupations for easy reference. However, the jobs of some employees may not be listed or you may not be able to find an exact match between the employee's job, or job title, and a job title in the **List of Occupational Groups & Titles**. In this case, find the job (job title) that most closely describes the type of work that the employee does. If there is doubt between two job titles it is better to select the one with the numerically lower worker functions codes. (The worker functions code is located to the left of each job title.) Because lower numbers equate with a higher skill level, this will help ensure that the employees' major skill areas will be covered.

5. Selection of the sections of the JSTNA which an employee must complete is the responsibility of the facilitator. Optimum value from the JSTNA will be obtained if facilitators use an employee's job description as the basis for selecting the appropriate sections. Because JSTNA scoring is done on a set basis (rather than a composite score for all sections) the number of sections completed by an employee is less important than the proper selection of sections to be completed.

   To the left of each job title in the **List of Occupational Groups & Titles** is the three digit worker functions code. These numbers correspond with the three digit codes established by the U.S. Department of Labor that indicate the complexity of a job relative to the other jobs described and evaluated in the DOT. As a general guideline, employees should compete at least those sections of the JSTNA indicated by the three digit code **plus** the next two lower skill level sections (those that have higher numbers than the three digit code). The exception is that employees in administrative, sales and technical-professional jobs do not have to complete section 7 of the **Things** category.

Thus, if an employee holds the position of **Drafter**, code 261, he or she should complete sections 2, 3 and 4 in the **Data** category; sections 6, 7 and 8 in the **People** category; and sections 1, 2 and 4 in the **Things** category.

6.   Once the facilitator has determined which sections of the JSTNA the employee should complete, he or she should distribute one copy of the JSTNA to all participating employees and ask them to write their name, actual job title and the codes for the sections that must be completed in the appropriate spaces on the front cover of the questionnaire.

7.   It is important that the employee answers each question honestly concentrating on whether further training is necessary in order to perform his or her job more effectively. The administrator should discourage employees from marking training needs solely on the basis of a desire to learn rather than on an actual need for training to improve job performance.

How to Score & Interpret the JSTNA

The JSTNA consists of 105 items that are allocated among three primary categories of worker functions: data, people and things. Each category is further subdivided into several sets of skill dimensions. Each skill dimension consists of five items. Respondents complete one or more sets of items in each of the three categories that are relevant to their particular occupational group.

Training needs can be identified in one of three ways; by a line item analysis of responses, by calculating scores for the various item sets, or by analyzing both set scores and line items. Each of the five alternatives in the response scale has been given a certain value as shown below. Note that two alternatives on the response scale, "**None**" and "**Not Applicable**," have point values of "0." In order to calculate set scores simply sum the point values of responses within each set. Set scores of 6 or more points strongly suggest that a training need exists for that particular skill dimension.

JSTNA response alternative point values:

> Very Considerably = 3
> Considerably = 2
> Somewhat = 1
> None = 0
> Not applicable = 0

The training needs threshold score of 6 points includes factoring for the possibility that up to two of the five set items may not be relevant to the employee's job. If three or more set items are not relevant then line item analysis is recommended instead of set score analysis in order to properly assess training needs.

When assessing a respondent's training needs facilitators, supervisors or counselors should be careful not to overlook training needs that might exist among the lower level worker functions. Sometimes lower level worker functions remain relevant and crucial to the performance of an employee's current, more complex job yet have grown "rusty" from infrequent use. For example, over reliance on the use of an electronic calculator or computer might adversely affect the skill of performing arithmetic calculations manually when needed.

Each employee's supervisor should review the JSTNA after it has been completed. Any areas of disagreement should be noted and discussed with the employee. Employees will be more committed to further training if consensus is reached about training needs. Supervisors should pay special attention to line items "**Not Applicable**" or for which training needs were deemed "**None**."

In regard to the former, the JSTNA can be a valuable tool in helping to clarify job responsibilities.

Scored information from the JSTNA should be compared with job elements detailed in an employee's job description. The measurement items in the JSTNA are phrased in terms that are congruent with the listing and description of job elements in the Dictionary of Occupational Titles referenced earlier. The job descriptions that have been prepared for employees in your organization may be worded somewhat differently. However, it should be reasonably easy to relate the two sets of job elements so that you can identify exactly where training will be most beneficial for your employees.

The next step is to use the JSTNA data as the basis for developing an employee training program. Look for trends and patterns of training needs among the majority of employees in various occupational groups within your organization. Categorize these needs into generic groups like **oral communication** and **listening skills, office machine operating skills, office arithmetic, customer complaint handling**, etc. Once this is done a training course outline, syllabus and eventually individual training module lesson plans can be developed.

APPENDIX A - LIST OF OCCUPATIONAL GROUPS & TITLES

ADMINISTRATIVE

Work duties for this category mainly consist of formulating and carrying out administrative principles, guidelines and techniques in a given organization. Occupations in this category will usually involve routine non-clerical tasks or a combination of clerical and administrative tasks. Occupations involving strictly clerical tasks are listed under the Clerical category.

162	Accountant	267	Human Resource Advisor
167	Accountant, Systems	267	Investment Analyst
167	Auditor	267	Job Analyst (Personnel Analyst)
267	Budget Analyst	167	Management Analyst (also Systems Analyst)
157	Buyer		
217	Claim Adjuster	167	Material Scheduler (Production Control Scheduler)
117	Contract Administrator (also project Administrator or Coordinator)	167	Production Planner (also Production Scheduler
117	Contract Specialist (also Contract Coordinator)	157	Purchasing Agent
267	Credit Analyst	267	Recruiter
207	Credit Counselor	267	Research Analyst (insurance)
267	Employee Relations Specialist	267	Researcher (economics, political science)
267	Estimator		

CLERICAL

Work duties for this category involve general office work. Clerical duties can be a combination of any of the following: taking dictation or shorthand, typing, minor administrative duties, maintaining records, transmitting, transcribing, filing, computing, compiling, data inputting and/or operating office equipment.

387	Advertising Clerk	367	Receptionist
382	Bookkeeper (also Statistical Clerk & Payroll Clerk)	367	Reservations Clerk (also Reservations Agent)
362	Claims Clerk(insurance)	362	Secretary
362	Clerk-Typist	687	Service Clerk
357	Collection Clerk	387	Shipping & Receiving Clerk (also Inventory Clerk)
362	Computer Operator		
362	Court Clerk	382	Statistical Clerk, Advertising
582	Data Entry Clerk	662	Telephone Operator
367	File Clerk	362	Teller
367	Hotel clerk (also front desk clerk)	267	Title Clerk
687	Mail Clerk (also Mail Handler)		
382	Production Clerk		
167	Production Coordinator (also material Coordinator, Production Expediter, Schedule Clerk, Progress Clerk, Scheduler)		

EDUCATION

Work duties for this category are primarily related to instructing others in the principles, techniques or application of a given academic or business subject. This category includes industrial and vocational education and education related occupations such as financial aids and student counselors or advisers.

167	Director of Student Affairs	227	Teacher, Learning Disabled
267	Evaluator	224	Teacher, Physically Impaired
227	Faculty Member, College or University	227	Teacher, Mentally Impaired
117	Financial Aids Officer	227	Teacher, Secondary School (also
107	Foreign Student Adviser		High School Teacher)
222	Instructor, Business Education	227	Teacher, Vocational Training
221	Instructor, Technical Training	227	Training Instructor (also
117	Public Health Educator		Training Representative)
227	Teacher, Elementary or Preschool	117	Vocational Rehabilitation Consultant

HEALTHCARE

Work duties for this category mainly involve services given for the prevention or treatment of physical or mental illnesses and for the promotion of good health. Included are all hospital workers except for those whose occupations are classified under **Administrative**, **Clerical**, or **Technical** (Professional and non-professional.) such as Human Relations Advisor, Secretary and Data Processing professionals.

124	Dietitian, Clinical	361	Respiratory Therapist
374	Emergency Medical Technologist	107	Speech Therapist
677	Food Server Worker, Hospital	362	Technician, Dialysis
687	Housekeeper, Hospital	362	Technician, EKG
362	Medical Assistant	374	Technician, Surgical
364	Nurse, General Duty	362	Technologist, Cardiovascular
127	Nurse, Infection Control	362	Technologist, CT
124	Nurse Instructor	364	Technologist, Echocardiograph
264	Nurse Practitioner	261	Technologist, Medical
261	Technologist, Medical	361	Technologist, Radiation Therapy
121	Occupational Therapist	362	Technologist, Radiologic
364	Paramedic	362	Technologist, Special Procedures
382	Pharmacist Technician/Clerk	364	Technologist, Ultrasound (also
364	Phlebotomist		Diagnostic Medical Sonographer)
121	Physical Therapist	362	Tumor Registrar
364	Physician Assistant		

SALES & RELATED

This category primarily involves influencing people in order to obtain purchase of a product or service. Includes occupations closely related to sales transactions even though the individual might not be present when the transaction actually takes place. Occupations that involve activities such as delivery, fulfillment, promotion, publicity, sales and service are also included in this category.

357	Advertising Sales Representative (also Advertising Solicitor)	477	Sales Clerk
167	Account Executive	367	Sales Correspondent (clerical)
362	Customer Service Representative	151	Sales Engineer
477	Deliverer, Merchandise (retail trade)	357	Salesperson, General Merchandise
353	Driver, Sales Route (also Delivery Route Truck Driver)	157	Sales Representative, Data Processing Services
067	Market Research Analyst I	257	Sales Representative, Dental & Medical Equipment
157	Pharmaceutical Detailer (wholesale)	357	Telemarketer (also Telephone Sales Representative)
167	Public Relations Representative		

TECHNICAL (Applies to both technical and technical-professional)

Work duties for this category involve the theoretical or practical aspects of fields such as engineering, architecture, science, mathematics, drafting, inspection and testing, laboratory, research, design and development, data processing and other technical fields. Usually these occupations require extensive educational preparation obtained from universities, junior colleges or technical schools.

Technical

261	Chemical Laboratory Technician	261	Radio Mechanic
261	Civil Engineering Technician	261	Research Mechanic (aircraft mfg.) (also Laboratory Test Mechanic)
262	Data Acquisition Lab Technician		
261	Data Communication Technician	167	School Plant Consultant (education)
362	Design Technician, Computer-Aided	364	Scientific Helper (also Laboratory Assistant; Research Assistant)
261	Drafter		
281	Drafter, Civil, Electronic or Electrical	161	Technician (Electrical, Electronics, Mechanical Engineering)
281	Drafter Assistant		
281	Laboratory Tester		

Technical-Professional

061	Aerodynamics Engineer		162	Programmer/Analyst
061	Architect		167	Quality Control Engineer
061	Biomedical, Chemical, Civil, Electrical, Electronics, Materials, Mechanical Engineer		161	Stress Analyst
			162	Systems Programmer
			162	Technical Operations Specialist
061	Chemist		262	User Support Analyst (also Help Desk Representative; Information Center Specialist; Office Automation Analyst)
261	Controls Project Engineer (also Controls Designer)			
067	Economist			
167	Field Service Engineer		167	Value Engineer (aircraft mfg.) (also Cost Development Engineer; Design Specialist)
167	Industrial, Manufacturing Engineer			
264	Microcomputer Support Specialist			

Participant Booklet for

JOB SKILLS TRAINING NEEDS ASSESSMENT

by Louis E. Tagliaferri, PhD

ED-101

ORGANIZATION:						
EMPLOYEE:						
JOB TITLE:						
CIRCLE THE JSTNA SECTIONS TO BE COMPLETED						
DATA:	0	1	2	3	4	5	6
PEOPLE:	0	1	2	5	6	7	8
THINGS:	0	1	2	4	5	6	7

Directions: Please carefully read all of the items in the sets that you have been asked to complete. Decide the extent to which you would benefit by receiving further training in the worker functions that are described. Think in terms of the positive effect that further training might have on your job performance and on your ability to do your job rather than whether you would simply enjoy further training. Indicate your decision by placing a mark in the appropriate column to the right of each item. If you believe that a particular worker function does not apply to your job at all, place a mark in the column marked **Not Applicable.**

To what extent would you benefit from additional training that will help you to:

	Very Considerably	Considerably	Somewhat	None	Not Applicable

Data 0

	Very Considerably	Considerably	Somewhat	None	Not Applicable
D. 01 Use creativity and originality to design or make improvements to products or services.	❏	❏	❏	❏	❏
D. 02 Conduct research to discover new uses for materials, products or designs or to develop solutions for complex problems.	❏	❏	❏	❏	❏
D. 03 Bring together and integrate information, concepts or ideas to formulate new or experimental designs, systems or products.	❏	❏	❏	❏	❏
D. 04 Interpret data and formulate hypotheses for the creative application of concepts and ideas.	❏	❏	❏	❏	❏
D. 05 Use specialized knowledge to discover facts or to make interpretations resulting from the analyses of data.	❏	❏	❏	❏	❏

Data 1

	Very Considerably	Considerably	Somewhat	None	Not Applicable
D. 11 Organize activities determining time, place, sequence of events and staffing requirements as needed.	❏	❏	❏	❏	❏
D. 12 Establish control measures to ensure that organizational goals and objectives are met.	❏	❏	❏	❏	❏
D. 13. Coordinate and direct various phases of projects and activities including the assignment of personnel and equipment as required.	❏	❏	❏	❏	❏
D. 14 Implement rules and regulations affecting planned work activities.	❏	❏	❏	❏	❏
D. 15 Authorize, direct and control the various tasks and activities necessary to produce products or provide services.	❏	❏	❏	❏	❏

Data 2

	Very Considerably	Considerably	Somewhat	None	Not Applicable
D. 21 Examine technical, scientific or other data in order to recommend courses of action.	❏	❏	❏	❏	❏
D. 22 Study documents and records to ensure conformance with policies, instructions or legal requirements.	❏	❏	❏	❏	❏
D. 23 Investigate and evaluate problems or complaints and attempt to find appropriate solutions.	❏	❏	❏	❏	❏
D. 24 Use analyzed data to develop of alternative ideas or actions.	❏	❏	❏	❏	❏
D. 25 Review and study reports to identify deviation or variance from norms.	❏	❏	❏	❏	❏

	Very Considerably	Considerably	Somewhat	None	Not Applicable

Data 3

D. 31   Summarize or classify information to be submitted for approval or review. ❏ ❏ ❏ ❏ ❏

D. 32   Gather, collate or classify information about data, people or things. ❏ ❏ ❏ ❏ ❏

D. 33   Maintain financial, operational, personnel or inventory records or data. ❏ ❏ ❏ ❏ ❏

D. 34   Review records and prepare reports pertaining to volume, costs, types or categories or other classifications. ❏ ❏ ❏ ❏ ❏

D. 35   Report compiled data or information and carry out prescribed actions. ❏ ❏ ❏ ❏ ❏

Data 4

D. 41   Calculate charges, costs, quantities or payments. ❏ ❏ ❏ ❏ ❏

D. 42   Enter data and operate computation equipment such as calculators, computers or other devices. ❏ ❏ ❏ ❏ ❏

D. 43   Collect payment and issue receipts or tickets to customers. ❏ ❏ ❏ ❏ ❏

D. 44   Calculate charges using charts and tables. ❏ ❏ ❏ ❏ ❏

D. 45   Figure and prepare quotes for charges, costs or fees. ❏ ❏ ❏ ❏ ❏

Data 5

D. 51   Transcribe verbal or written data or information to punch cards, typewriter, computer or any other recording device. ❏ ❏ ❏ ❏ ❏

D. 52   Copy or enter information on a document or form. ❏ ❏ ❏ ❏ ❏

D. 53   Type letters, forms or other documents. ❏ ❏ ❏ ❏ ❏

D. 54   Post information such as quantities, volume, temperature or meter readings in appropriate forms or ledgers. ❏ ❏ ❏ ❏ ❏

D. 55   Transfer information or data from original source to forms, records or reports. ❏ ❏ ❏ ❏ ❏

Data 6

D. 61   Sort or stack products, material or documents following a specific sequence. ❏ ❏ ❏ ❏ ❏

D. 62   Proof read or otherwise check printed or written material or documents to ensure accuracy and correctness. ❏ ❏ ❏ ❏ ❏

		Very Considerably	Considerably	Somewhat	None	Not Applicable
D. 63	Inspect documents, boxes or containers to verify accuracy of printed or written information.	❏	❏	❏	❏	❏
D. 64	Examine the physical condition of products, materials or supplies to ensure compliance with quality standards or other guidelines.	❏	❏	❏	❏	❏
D. 65	Perform clerical duties such as filing, sorting or collating.	❏	❏	❏	❏	❏

•••••••••••••••••••••••••••••••••••••

People 0

P .01	Render consultation to those in physical or emotional distress.	❏	❏	❏	❏	❏
P. 02	Work out plans and strategies with individuals or organizations for overcoming social, technical or economic problems.	❏	❏	❏	❏	❏
P. 03	Advise and assist individuals in the solution of problems that require legal, scientific, clinical or other professional expertise.	❏	❏	❏	❏	❏
P. 04	Guide individuals to find solutions to their own problems.	❏	❏	❏	❏	❏
P. 05	Share knowledge and expertise to help develop the personal and professional capabilities of individuals.	❏	❏	❏	❏	❏

People 1

P. 11	Confer with others to reach agreement about matters such as policies, programs or contracts.	❏	❏	❏	❏	❏
P. 12	Exchange ideas, information and opinions with others to arrive at mutually agreed solutions, decisions or conclusions.	❏	❏	❏	❏	❏
P. 13	Meet with others to arrange terms of contracts and fees.	❏	❏	❏	❏	❏
P. 14	Negotiate for the rental or purchase of merchandise, materials or services.	❏	❏	❏	❏	❏
P. 15	Use research data to prepare negotiating positions and strategies.	❏	❏	❏	❏	❏

People 2

	Very Considerably	Considerably	Somewhat	None	Not Applicable
P. 21 Prepare instructional material including audio/visual aids.	❏	❏	❏	❏	❏
P. 22 Conduct classes and present instructional material.	❏	❏	❏	❏	❏
P. 23 Use various teaching techniques such as lecture, case study, demonstration and group discussion.	❏	❏	❏	❏	❏
P. 24 Understand the theory and principles of learning.	❏	❏	❏	❏	❏
P. 25 Observe and evaluate learning comprehension of students or employees.	❏	❏	❏	❏	❏

People 5

	Very Considerably	Considerably	Somewhat	None	Not Applicable
P. 51 Promote use of products or services.	❏	❏	❏	❏	❏
P. 52 Persuade others to accept a certain idea or point of view.	❏	❏	❏	❏	❏
P. 53 Contact individuals or organizations in person, by telephone or by other means to solicit business.	❏	❏	❏	❏	❏
P. 54 Influence others to buy products or to use services.	❏	❏	❏	❏	❏
P. 55 Present and explain selling features of products or services.	❏	❏	❏	❏	❏

People 6

	Very Considerably	Considerably	Somewhat	None	Not Applicable
P. 61 Give instructions or directions to helpers, assistants or patients.	❏	❏	❏	❏	❏
P. 62 Offer ideas and suggestions for improvement.	❏	❏	❏	❏	❏
P. 63 Answer requests for information from customers, patients or employees.	❏	❏	❏	❏	❏
P. 64 Respond to complaints or suggestions from customers, patients or employees.	❏	❏	❏	❏	❏
P. 65 Conduct interviews to obtain information from customers, patients or employees.	❏	❏	❏	❏	❏

People 7

	Very Considerably	Considerably	Somewhat	None	Not Applicable
P. 71 Obtain or receive merchandise, material or supplies.	❏	❏	❏	❏	❏
P. 72 Issue or distribute merchandise, material or supplies.	❏	❏	❏	❏	❏
P. 73 Receive payment or issue receipts for merchandise, material or supplies.	❏	❏	❏	❏	❏
P.74 Attend to the needs or requests of patients, customers or employees.	❏	❏	❏	❏	❏

	Very Considerably	Considerably	Somewhat	None	Not Applicable

P. 75 Render a variety of personal, business or social services to patients, customers or employees. ☐ ☐ ☐ ☐ ☐

People 8

P. 81 Understand job duties and responsibilities. ☐ ☐ ☐ ☐ ☐

P. 82 Show ability to follow job instructions. ☐ ☐ ☐ ☐ ☐

P. 83 Demonstrate willingness to accept job responsibilities and instructions. ☐ ☐ ☐ ☐ ☐

P. 84 Help and assist other workers when requested. ☐ ☐ ☐ ☐ ☐

P. 85 Understand job performance standards. ☐ ☐ ☐ ☐ ☐

•••••••••••••••••••••••••••••••••••••

Things 0

T. 01 Operate highly technical equipment, observe operations and verify that output meets specifications. ☐ ☐ ☐ ☐ ☐

T. 02 Adjust settings on equipment or machines so that they perform as designed. ☐ ☐ ☐ ☐ ☐

T. 03 Set up, calibrate, or adjust equipment, start operations and check initial output for accuracy. ☐ ☐ ☐ ☐ ☐

T. 04 Use knowledge of operations to determine equipment set up requirements. ☐ ☐ ☐ ☐ ☐

T. 05 Monitor operation of equipment and make adjustments or replacement of parts in order to ensure proper functioning. ☐ ☐ ☐ ☐ ☐

Things 1

T. 11 Diagnose malfunctions in operation of equipment or machines using specialized test equipment. ☐ ☐ ☐ ☐ ☐

T. 12 Use knowledge of process or operations to prepare drawings, models, sketches or designs. ☐ ☐ ☐ ☐ ☐

T. 13 Measure, mark, lay out, or work designs to achieve desired precision. ☐ ☐ ☐ ☐ ☐

T. 14 Position equipment, laboratory tools or other objects so that precision performance can be attained. ☐ ☐ ☐ ☐ ☐

	Very Considerably	Considerably	Somewhat	None	Not Applicable
T. 15 Use independent judgement to select the proper tools, equipment or other work aids for the specific task to be performed.	❏	❏	❏	❏	❏

Things 2

T. 21 Start, stop and control operations of equipment or machines.	❏	❏	❏	❏	❏
T. 22 Adjust progress and setting of equipment or machines.	❏	❏	❏	❏	❏
T. 23 Observe dials, gauges, settings or other devices in order to regulate operation of equipment or machines.	❏	❏	❏	❏	❏
T. 24 Observe, record and report performance information about equipment or machines.	❏	❏	❏	❏	❏
T. 25 Turn controls, depress keys, move levers or otherwise operate equipment or machines.	❏	❏	❏	❏	❏

Things 4

T. 41 Use hands or mechanical equipment to perform operations like applying pressure, turning, or elevating.	❏	❏	❏	❏	❏
T. 42 Move, guide, place or position objects, material or patients.	❏	❏	❏	❏	❏
T. 43 Insert objects like letters or other documents into envelopes.	❏	❏	❏	❏	❏
T. 44 Select appropriate tools, equipment, objects or other work aids that are required to perform a job.	❏	❏	❏	❏	❏
T. 45 Use hands or mechanical equipment to sort, collate, fold, or perform similar operations.	❏	❏	❏	❏	❏

Things 5

T. 51 Start, stop and observe the functioning of equipment or machines.	❏	❏	❏	❏	❏
T. 52 Observe equipment operations to detect malfunctions.	❏	❏	❏	❏	❏
T. 53 Make adjustments to control equipment.	❏	❏	❏	❏	❏
T. 54 Regulate output of automatic equipment or machines by controlling speed, flow, temperature or pressure.	❏	❏	❏	❏	❏
T. 55 Monitor quality of output of equipment or machines.	❏	❏	❏	❏	❏

Things 6

	Very Considerably	Considerably	Somewhat	None	Not Applicable
T. 61 Insert or remove paper, stock, film or other material into or from machines.	❏	❏	❏	❏	❏
T. 62 Place material into bins or trays for processing.	❏	❏	❏	❏	❏
T. 63 Unload paper, cards, tape, disks or other objects from machines after processing is completed.	❏	❏	❏	❏	❏
T. 64 Load or unload objects from moving conveyor system.	❏	❏	❏	❏	❏
T. 65 Remove and collect material that has been processed in equipment or machines.	❏	❏	❏	❏	❏

Things 7

	Very Considerably	Considerably	Somewhat	None	Not Applicable
T. 71 Load, push and unload hand trucks or wheeled containers.	❏	❏	❏	❏	❏
T. 72 Tag, tie, bundle, wrap or package material.	❏	❏	❏	❏	❏
T. 73 Distribute papers, cards, mail, notices, packages or other material.	❏	❏	❏	❏	❏
T. 74 Lift objects and place in racks, bins or cabinets.	❏	❏	❏	❏	❏
T. 75 Transport, move or file material manually or with mechanical aid.	❏	❏	❏	❏	❏

Leadership
Effectiveness Profile

by
Louis E. Tagliaferri, Ph.D.

Administration Guide
MD-104

WHAT IT IS

The Leadership Effectiveness Profile (LEP) gives supervisors and managers important feedback about (a) their leadership styles, (b) their ability to correctly assess situations that require leadership behavior, (c) the extent to which they are willing to modify or adopt their leadership behavior to that which is most effective in a given situation, and (d) their overall leadership effectiveness. The LEP can be used by individual managers and supervisors for self-assessment purposes. However, optimum value will be obtained when it is used in its multi-level format; i.e. ratings also by the superior and by the subordinates or peers.

The LEP is based upon well established management principles. For several decades management scientists have tried to determine what the most effective leadership style is. In the 1950's McGregor (1) presented his answer to this question in the form of the well known Theory X and Theory Y. Rensis Likert (2) suggested that participative management was in most cases the best, most effective leadership style available to managers. Blake and Mouton (3) identified eighty-one different leadership styles. They concluded that the most effective leaders were those, who, in decision making and related behavior, were equally people and task (production) oriented.

The most current theories of leadership, Hersey and Blanchard (4), Fiedler (5) and others suggests that there is no one best leadership style for all occasions. Rather, the most effective leaders is the person who has facility with a range of leadership styles; who can assess a situation requiring leadership behavior and determine which leadership style is best for that particular situation; and who can then modify or adapt his or her leadership behavior as appropriate.

Associated with this contingency or situational theory of leadership is a definition of up to five major leadership styles as follows:

Directive: The leader maintains tight control over the subordinate's task performance. Work standards are unilaterally set by the leader who also makes all or most of the job related decisions. Communication is mostly one-way, downward. Motivation relies on extrinsic rewards. Heavy reliance is placed on power of authority.

Persuasive: Very similar to directive. The major difference is that the persuasive leader prefers to "sell" (rather that "order") the subordinate on the merits of complying with the leader's decisions.

Consultative: The leader and subordinates function as equal members of a team. Decisions are made with the consensus of the team rather than only by the leader. Heavy emphasis is placed on intrinsic motivation. Communication is among all team members. The leader exercises normal control because the team is self-directed toward task accomplishment.

Participative: The leader and subordinates become jointly involved in most major aspects of their work. Decision making is a shared responsibility. Communication freely flows two-ways. Motivation is primarily intrinsic in nature supported by external rewards.

Delegative: The leader essentially becomes disassociated from the tasks and from task performers once delegation is made. Control is limited to results reporting by subordinates. The motivational climate permits subordinates to self-achieve motivation. What little communication is required is two-way in nature. Decisions are made by subordinates.

The effective leader will have skill in using all of these leadership styles. Depending upon the nature of the task to be accomplished, the expertise, skill, job and psychological maturity of subordinates, and upon situational variables like time parameters, the need for creativity, resistance to change, etc., the effective leader will select among the above to choose the most appropriate leadership style.

It should be kept in mind that different employees within the same work group respond to different leadership styles. A certain individual might respond best to a directive style today but will require a different leadership style as the task, his or her own behavior and the situation changes. The same principle, of course, applies to groups.

HOW TO SCORE & INTERPRET IT

A reproducible scoring form will be found on the next page of this guide. Photocopy reproduction is permitted to enable you to reproduce one scoring form for each employee who is being assessed. (Scoring and interpretation guidelines continue on the page following the scoring form.)

REPRODUCIBLE LEP SCORING FORM

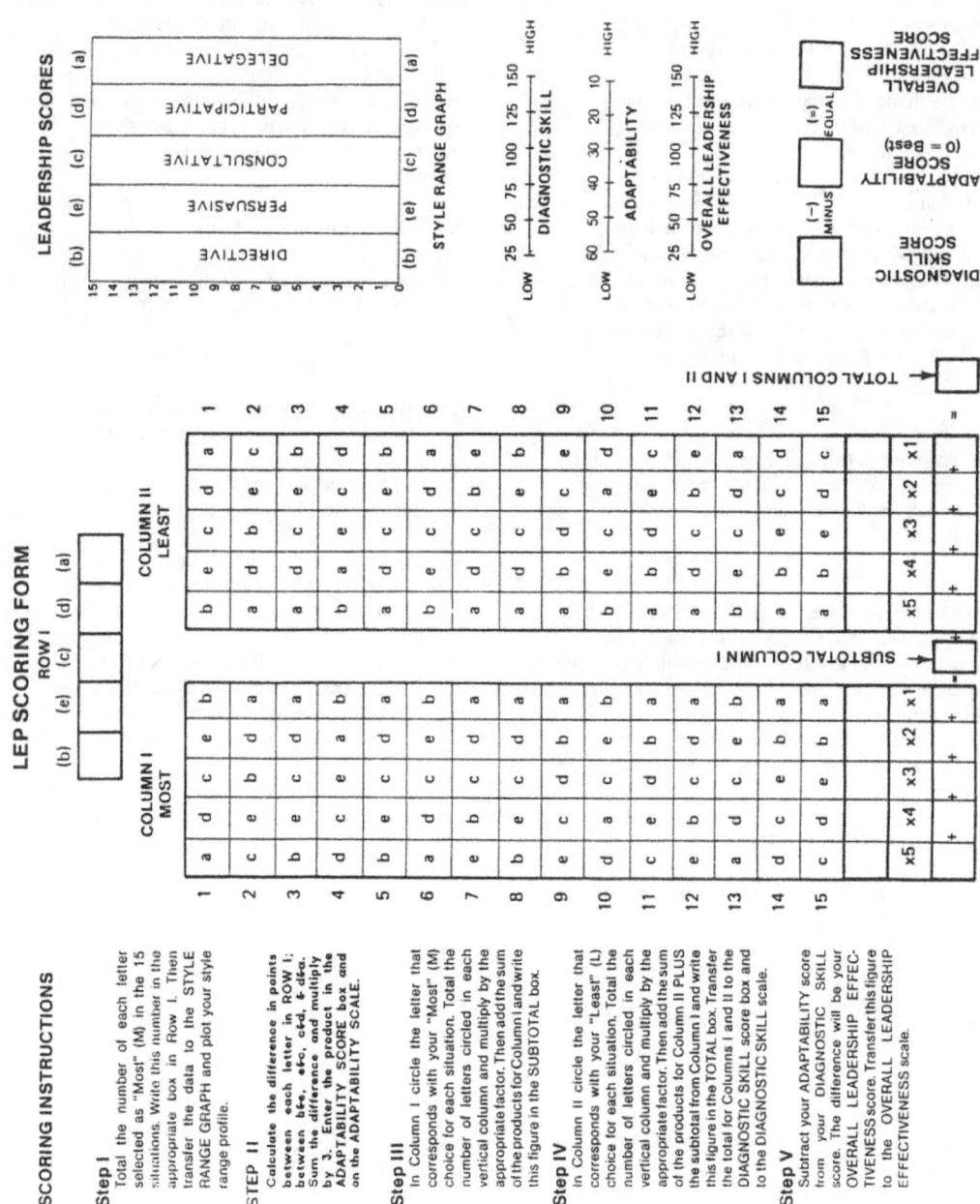

LEADERSHIP SCORES

(b)	(e)	(c)	(d)	(a)
DIRECTIVE	PERSUASIVE	CONSULTATIVE	PARTICIPATIVE	DELEGATIVE

STYLE RANGE GRAPH

DIAGNOSTIC SKILL
LOW 25 50 75 100 125 150 HIGH

ADAPTABILITY
LOW 60 50 40 30 20 10 HIGH

OVERALL LEADERSHIP EFFECTIVENESS
LOW 25 50 75 100 125 150 HIGH

DIAGNOSTIC SKILL SCORE (−) MINUS

ADAPTABILITY SCORE (0 = Best) (=) EQUAL

OVERALL LEADERSHIP EFFECTIVENESS SCORE

LEP SCORING FORM

ROW I

| (b) | (e) | (c) | (d) | (a) |

COLUMN I — MOST

1	a	d	c	e	b
2	c	e	d	d	a
3	b	b	b	d	a
4	d	c	e	c	b
5	b	e	c	d	a
6	a	d	c	e	b
7	e	b	c	d	a
8	b	e	c	d	a
9	e	c	d	e	a
10	d	a	e	c	a
11	c	e	d	b	a
12	e	b	e	d	a
13	a	d	c	e	b
14	c	c	e	c	a
15	c	d	e	e	a
	x5	x4	x3	x2	x1

SUBTOTAL COLUMN I

COLUMN II — LEAST

1	a	d	c	e	b
2	c	e	b	d	a
3	b	e	c	d	a
4	d	e	e	d	b
5	c	c	e	a	a
6	a	d	c	d	b
7	e	d	c	e	a
8	e	b	d	e	a
9	e	e	c	d	a
10	d	c	c	b	b
11	c	e	d	e	a
12	e	e	c	b	a
13	a	d	c	d	b
14	c	c	e	c	b
15	c	d	e	b	a
	x1	x2	x3	x4	x5

TOTAL COLUMNS I AND II

SCORING INSTRUCTIONS

Step I
Total the number of each letter selected as "Most" (M) in the 15 situations. Write this number in the appropriate box in Row I. Then transfer the data to the STYLE RANGE GRAPH and plot your style range profile.

STEP II
Calculate the difference in points between each letter in ROW I; between b&e, e&c, c&d, & d&a. Sum the difference and multiply by 3. Enter the product in the ADAPTABILITY SCORE box and on the ADAPTABILITY SCALE.

Step III
In Column I circle the letter that corresponds with your "Most" (M) choice for each situation. Total the number of letters circled in each vertical column and multiply by the appropriate factor. Then add the sum of the products for Column I and write this figure in the SUBTOTAL box.

Step IV
In Column II circle the letter that corresponds with your "Least" (L) choice for each situation. Total the number of letters circled in each vertical column and multiply by the appropriate factor. Then add the sum of the products for Column II PLUS the subtotal from Column I and write this figure in the TOTAL box. Transfer the total for Columns I and II to the DIAGNOSTIC SKILL score box and to the DIAGNOSTIC SKILL scale.

Step V
Subtract your ADAPTABILITY score from your DIAGNOSTIC SKILL score. The difference will be your OVERALL LEADERSHIP EFFECTIVENESS score. Transfer this figure to the OVERALL LEADERSHIP EFFECTIVENESS scale.

If you are a facilitator who will be administering the LEP to others we suggest that you first complete a LEP, yourself, and score it. This will help you to become familiar with the scoring process.

After you have scored your own LEP read the following descriptions of the LEP's various components:

STYLE RANGE GRAPH

This graph indicates the reliance that a manager places on each of the five basic leadership styles measured by the LEP.

Most managers have one leadership style with which they are most comfortable and a second back-up style with which they also have reasonable facility. In order to be most successful, however, a manager should also develop sufficient facility with alternative leadership styles so that he/she can use them effectively when the situation requires.

DIAGNOSTIC SKILL

This score indicates the extent to which a manager can correctly determine which leadership style is appropriate for a particular situation.

ADAPTABILITY

The adaptability score indicates the extent to which a manager is able to modify his/her leadership behavior in order to effectively deal with a particular employee behavior situation. Managers who are skilled using alternative leadership styles and who have good diagnostic skills usually can modify or adapt their leadership behavior as required in order to be most effective.

OVERALL LEADERSHIP EFFECTIVENESS

This score is based on the sum and product of the above component scores.

NORMATIVE DATA

STYLE RANGE	NORM	RECOMMENDED
Directive	3.24	2.0
Persuasive	1.47	2.0
Consultative	1.87	4.0
Participative	6.04	4.0
Delegative	1.99	3.0

Mean **Diagnostic Skill Score** is 118. Mean **Adaptability Score** is 45. Mean **Overall Leadership Effectiveness Score** is 74.

Normative data is based on scores from 200 managers and supervisors in both commercial and industrial organizations.

HOW TO ADMINISTER IT

Introduce the LEP by explaining its purpose and the objectives of the particular activity in which it is being administered. Be sure that you have a sufficient supply for all who will be completing the LEP. One LEP questionnaire is required for each person who is participating in the assessment. This includes the person who is being assessed, his/her superior and subordinates or peers, if you are using the multi-level format.

Allow 30-40 minutes for completion.

When scoring the LEP in multi-level use, average the scores of the subordinates or peers.

REFERENCES

(1) McGregor, Douglas, The Human Side of Enterprise, New York, McGraw-Hill, 1960.

(2) Likert, Rensis, New Patterns of Management, New York, McGraw-Hill, 1961.

(3) Blake, Robert R. and Mouton, Jane S., The Managerial Grid, Houston, Gulf Publishing Company, 1964.

(4) Hersey, Paul and Blanchard, Kenneth, Management of Organizational Behavior: Utilizing Human Resources, Englewood Cliffs, NJ, Prentice-Hall, 1977.

(5) Fiedler, Fred and Chemers, Martin, Improving Leadership Effectiveness, New York, John Wiley & Sons, Inc., 1984.

Leadership
Effectiveness Profile

by

Louis E. Tagliaferri, Ph.D.

Participant Booklet
MD-104

Organization:
Name:
You Are:
☐ The Above Person
☐ A Subordinate/Peer of the Above Person
☐ The Superior of the Above Person

INSTRUCTIONS

Directions: Below are fifteen (15) situations that any leader might encounter. Following each situation are five (5) alternative courses of action that a leader might take in order to deal with the situation. Read each situation carefully. Assume that the person whose name appears on the front cover of this questionnaire is the leader in each situation. Place an "M" in the space to the left of the alternative that you think this person would most likely take. Then place an "L" in the space to the left of the alternative that you think this person would least likely take.

1. You have been working participatively with your subordinates to solve various department problems. They have demonstrated proficiency and mature judgment. They ask you to help them solve a new problem.

    _____ a. Leave the group alone to solve the problem themselves.
    _____ b. Redefine job standards, goals and responsibilities. Supervise the group closely.
    _____ c. Obtain input from the group. Then develop a solution to the group to follow.
    _____ d. Work with the group to analyze the problem and develop a satisfactory solution.
    _____ e. Develop a solution to the problem and persuade the group to follow it.

2. Certain problems have developed among a group of your subordinates who have demonstrated a moderate degree of proficiency and responsibility. You are not sure whether you have given this group enough guidance in the past.

    _____ a. Leave the group alone to solve the problem themselves.
    _____ b. Redefine job standards, goals and responsibilities. Supervise the group closely.
    _____ c. Obtain input from the group. Then develop a solution for the group to follow.
    _____ d. Work with the group to analyze the problem and develop a satisfactory solution.
    _____ e. Develop a solution to the problem and persuade the group to follow it.

3. Your work group has not been responding to your friendly efforts to encourage performance improvement. A "country club" atmosphere seems to exist. A difficult work problem has now arisen.

    _____ a. Leave the group alone to solve the problem themselves.
    _____ b. Redefine job standards, goals and responsibilities. Supervise the group closely.
    _____ c. Obtain input from the group. Then develop a solution for the group to follow.
    _____ d. Work with the group to analyze the problem and develop a satisfactory solution.
    _____ e. Develop a solution to the problem and persuade the group to follow it.

4. Members of your work group have demonstrated maturity, proficiency and responsibility. A major systems change will soon be introduced in your department and you anticipate that some problems will be caused by the staff reassignments that it requires.

    _____ a. Leave the group alone to solve the problem themselves.
    _____ b. Redefine job standards, goals and responsibilities. Supervise the group closely.
    _____ c. Obtain input from the group. Then develop a solution for the group to follow.
    _____ d. Work with the group to analyze the problem and develop a satisfactory solution.
    _____ e. Develop a solution to the problem and persuade the group to follow it.

5. **The pleasant relationships within your new department are marred by a history of poor performance. The problem must be solved promptly.**

_____ a. Leave the group alone to solve the problem themselves.
_____ b. Redefine job standards, goals and responsibilities. Supervise the group closely.
_____ c. Obtain input from the group. Then develop a solution for the group to follow.
_____ d. Work with the group to analyze the problem and develop a satisfactory solution.
_____ e. Develop a solution to the problem and persuade the group to follow it.

6. **A serious problem has just arisen in your newly assigned work unit. Your subordinates are experienced, proficient and work well together as a team. The unit has a good performance history.**

_____ a. Leave the group alone to solve the problem themselves.
_____ b. Redefine job standards, goals and responsibilities. Supervise the group closely.
_____ c. Obtain input from the group. Then develop a solution for the group to follow.
_____ d. Work with the group to analyze the problem and develop a satisfactory solution.
_____ e. Develop a solution to the problem and persuade the group to follow it.

7. **You have recently introduced a new operating system in your work unit. A group of employees whose marginal performance you want to improve are resisting the change. Their performance continues to decline.**

_____ a. Leave the group alone to solve the problem themselves.
_____ b. Redefine job standards, goals and responsibilities. Supervise the group closely.
_____ c. Obtain input from the group. Then develop a solution for the group to follow.
_____ d. Work with the group to analyze the problem and develop a satisfactory solution.
_____ e. Develop a solution to the problem and persuade the group to follow it.

8. **Your work group seems to be confused. Many employees in the group are new and are relatively inexperienced. Work group performance is poor.**

_____ a. Leave the group alone to solve the problem themselves.
_____ b. Redefine job standards, goals and responsibilities. Supervise the group closely.
_____ c. Obtain input from the group. Then develop a solution for the group to follow.
_____ d. Work with the group to analyze the problem and develop a satisfactory solution.
_____ e. Develop a solution to the problem and persuade the group to follow it.

9. **A group of employees within your department who had formerly been marginal performers seem to be improving. They are currently having difficulty with new work methods recently introduced into the unit.**

_____ a. Leave the group alone to solve the problem themselves.
_____ b. Redefine job standards, goals and responsibilities. Supervise the group closely.
_____ c. Obtain input from the group. Then develop a solution for the group to follow.
_____ d. Work with the group to analyze the problem and develop a satisfactory solution.
_____ e. Develop a solution to the problem and persuade the group to follow it.

10. **You have been assigned to solve an operational problem in your work group. A great deal of creativity will be required in order to deal with the problem issue. Your subordinates are mature and experienced.**

_____ a. Leave the group alone to solve the problem themselves.
_____ b. Redefine job standards, goals and responsibilities. Supervise the group closely.
_____ c. Obtain input from the group. Then develop a solution for the group to follow.
_____ d. Work with the group to analyze the problem and develop a satisfactory solution.
_____ e. Develop a solution to the problem and persuade the group to follow it.

11. **Members of your work group have been responding to your constructive efforts to improve their performance. A minor problem has developed, however, and you must ensure that the group does not "backslide."**

_____ a. Leave the group alone to solve the problem themselves.
_____ b. Redefine job standards, goals and responsibilities. Supervise the group closely.
_____ c. Obtain input from the group. Then develop a solution for the group to follow.
_____ d. Work with the group to analyze the problem and develop a satisfactory solution.
_____ e. Develop a solution to the problem and persuade the group to follow it.

12. **Relationships among you and your subordinates are good. They have a moderate degree of proficiency but still are not performing at the level that you expect. They seem to be struggling with a work problem.**

_____ a. Leave the group alone to solve the problem themselves.
_____ b. Redefine job standards, goals and responsibilities. Supervise the group closely.
_____ c. Obtain input from the group. Then develop a solution for the group to follow.
_____ d. Work with the group to analyze the problem and develop a satisfactory solution.
_____ e. Develop a solution to the problem and persuade the group to follow it.

13. **The employees in your work group have demonstrated a high degree of proficiency and responsibility. A project involving a technical problem of a type that they have previously experienced has now arisen.**

_____ a. Leave the group alone to solve the problem themselves.
_____ b. Redefine job standards, goals and responsibilities. Supervise the group closely.
_____ c. Obtain input from the group. Then develop a solution for the group to follow.
_____ d. Work with the group to analyze the problem and develop a satisfactory solution.
_____ e. Develop a solution to the problem and persuade the group to follow it.

14. **You have been accustomed to letting your subordinates work out various problems for themselves. Lately, however, they seem to be having difficulty solving problems that affect them as a work group.**

_____ a. Leave the group alone to solve the problem themselves.
_____ b. Redefine job standards, goals and responsibilities. Supervise the group closely.
_____ c. Obtain input from the group. Then develop a solution for the group to follow.
_____ d. Work with the group to analyze the problem and develop a satisfactory solution.
_____ e. Develop a solution to the problem and persuade the group to follow it.

15. **You have had a practice of working with your subordinates to develop solutions to operational problems. One of the problems that your work group now faces is significantly more complicated than those that they have dealt with in the past. The problem must be solved quickly.**

_____ a. Leave the group alone to solve the problem themselves.
_____ b. Redefine job standards, goals and responsibilities. Supervise the group closely.
_____ c. Obtain input from the group. Then develop a solution for the group to follow.
_____ d. Work with the group to analyze the problem and develop a satisfactory solution.
_____ e. Develop a solution to the problem and persuade the group to follow it.

Leadership Skills Test

by
Louis E. Tagliaferri, Ph.D.

Administration Guide
MD-127ELG

Overview

The Talico Inc. Leadership Skills Test (LST) is a developmental assessment and feedback instrument designed to evaluate leadership training needs for employees at any level of an organization. The instrument is based on current management and leadership research findings and other literature that identify which work related practices and behaviors must be exercised in the modern work place in order to influence today's employees to achieve their full performance potential. Some of these leadership behaviors and practices are in sharp contrast with the earlier concept that leadership can most effectively be exercised through the process of direction, control and reward. Instead, the general consensus today is that in order to be as effective as possible leaders must demonstrate proficiency in the following ten sets of behaviors or practices:

Coaching	Facilitating	Servicing Customers
Communicating	Influencing	Solution Finding
Empowering	Managing Change	Team Building
	Managing Projects	

The LST evaluates the extent that a person's beliefs and perceptions are congruent with attributes within each of the above measurement dimensions. A description of these skill dimensions will be found in the Test Answers and Skill Dimensions section of this guide.

The rationale for the test is based on the premise that people usually behave in a way that is congruent with their attitude and beliefs. By measuring an individual's attitude and beliefs about leadership it is possible to assess the likelihood that in a leadership role a person will behave in a particular way. The LST requires respondents to differentiate between two forms of leadership related behavior, a classical or traditional form and a modern form. Respondents whose attitudes and beliefs about leadership are congruent with modern leadership behavior and practices will usually select the LST item that is most consistent with their understanding and perceptions. In a leadership role the same individual will more likely behave in a way that is congruent with the behavior of a modern leader than in a way that is congruent with the behavior of a traditional leader.

Description

The test consists of 40 paired comparison sets distributed among the above 10 skill dimensions. LST items are in the form of behaviors and practices that might apply to the role of a leader in any organization. All of the behaviors and practices are typical of those frequently demonstrated by organizational leaders, but only certain among them are typical of the modern leader. Respondents are required to choose which item in each pair they believe is <u>more</u> characteristic than the other of the behavior or practice of a modern leader.

The test requires only 15 to 20 minutes to complete. It can be entirely self-administered and self-scored using the manual scoring format in this guide. Alternatively, easy-to-use spreadsheet software is usually readily available and simplifies the collection, analysis and reporting of test results. This is especially helpful when the test is administered to larger populations.

The product of the test is a profile in the form of a chart that identifies leadership development needs in each skill dimension and that also provides a composite score for the test as a whole. Development needs identification is a function of the number of items selected in each skill dimension that are congruent with modern leadership research findings. A lower score generally indicates a higher development need.

Application

The LST has many possible applications among employees at any level of the organization. It can be used as a training needs analysis tool for employees who currently hold managerial or supervisory positions or for non-supervisory employees who are candidates for those responsibilities. The LST is also ideal for helping to identify employees who have the potential for leadership roles in self-directed work teams, continuous improvement teams or in any other work activity in which an employee must exercise leadership behavior.

The LST can also serve as a learning instrument in a leadership training class. Trainers can use the LST to provide feedback to class participants about their leadership beliefs, behaviors and practices. The LST can also be used as a stand alone performance coaching tool.

Administration

The first and most important step in successfully administering the LST is to ensure that test participants clearly understand the test's purpose and objectives and how you intend to use the test scores. You should inform test participants that the LST has been designed as a developmental tool, to help identify training and development needs for employees who either are currently in a leadership role or who are candidates for a leadership role. You should explain that the test scores are not performance indicators but rather are indicators of developmental opportunities that can enhance a person's leadership ability.

If you prefer, the LST can be entirely self-administered and self-scored by an individual. Proctored testing is strictly optional. For scoring and profiling purposes you may photocopy the Test Answers and Skill Dimensions and the Leadership Skills Chart that is included with this booklet. One set of this material is required in order to score and interpret each test. For self-scoring purposes, distribute one copy of the set to each test participant after he or she has completed the test. You may still choose to distribute one copy of the set to test participants if you use a spreadsheet software to score the test because that type of software would not produce a copy of the Leadership Skills Chart, which is a useful graphic presentation of an individual's development needs.

LEADERSHIP SKILLS CHART

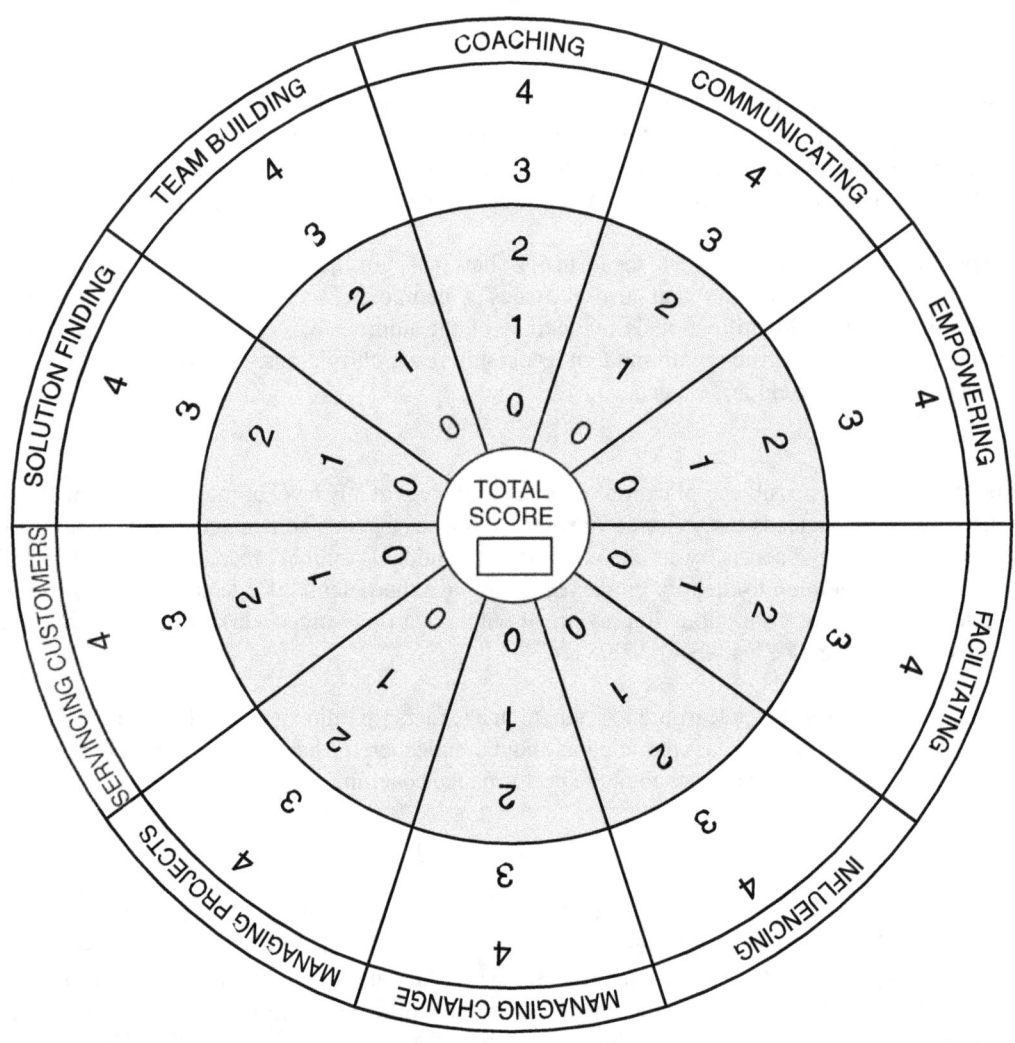

HIGH	LEADERSHIP DEVELOPMENT NEED	LOW

```
|0 • • • • • • • • •10 • • • • • • • • •20 • • • • • • • • •30 • • • • • • • •40 |
```

LOW	CONGRUENCE WITH EFFECTIVE LEADERSHIP BEHAVIOR	HIGH

INSTRUCTIONS: The answers for the Leadership Skills Test are on the next page of this guide. Circle the number of items that you answered correctly in each dimension of the above Leadership Skills Chart. Circled numbers that fall within the shaded section (0, 1, or 2) indicate that you may have a development need in that particular leadership skill dimension.

Next, write the total of correct answers both in the Total Score box and also in the congruence scale that is found immediately below the chart. This score shows the extent that your overall leadership behaviors and practices are congruent with those required of leaders in today's work force and also the extent that you may have an overall leadership skill development need.

Test Answers and Skill Dimensions

Below is a list of the leadership skill dimensions that the LST evaluates. The numbers in parenthesis indicate those answers which are most congruent with modern leadership behavior and practices.

Coaching: (02a) (14b) (22b) (40a)

Improving the competencies and commitment of employees through a process of coaching that employs the functions of counseling, mentoring, tutoring and confronting with respect to problems and situations that can affect their job performance.

Communicating: (11b) (26b) (33b) (38b)

Establishing and maintaining open, two-way communication with employees that provides them with essential job related information and obtains feedback about their problems, concerns and suggestions.

Empowering: (06a) (12b) (16a) (20a)

Developing the competencies and influence of employees, both as individuals and as teams of individuals, in a way that involves shared responsibility, shared rewards and a focus on meeting performance objectives.

Facilitating: (25a) (34a) (35b) (37a)

Intervening in the work activities of employees for the purpose of helping them to increase their full performance potential, to solve work related problems and to achieve their performance objectives. Strengthening employees by providing resources, clarifying roles and norms and helping them develop effective work processes.

Influencing: (03a) (09a) (17b) (30b)

Achieving leader acceptance and willing followers by using the process of influence based on the power of expertise and referent power, by inspiring and by creating challenging, achievable goals for employees.

Managing Change: (07a) (10b) (15a) (19b)

Being an effective agent for change by focusing on goal attainment and maintaining a sense of control during periods of uncertainty while at the same time demonstrating flexibility and adaptability. Preparing employees to respond to change in a constructive way.

Managing Projects: (08b) (31b) (36a) (39a)

Envisioning future events and developing strategies for dealing with them. Being able to develop project plans, train and develop project team skills and establish and follow appropriate project control measures to ensure goal attainment.

Servicing Customers: (04b) (13a) (29a) (32b)

Providing quality service to both internal and external customers. Committing oneself and one's team to meeting all of the customer's needs and expectations. Using customer feedback for purposes of continuous improvement.

Solution Finding: (18a) (21b) (23a) (28b)

Defining the problem and understanding the real problem or decision issue. Effectively using both creative and rational problem solving skills in a way that assures full inclusion of all members of the team.

Team Building: (01a) (05a) (24b) (27b)

Accomplishing performance objectives through effective teamwork. Building teams by training employees in team skills, encouraging team interaction and by facilitating team development through open feedback and constructive critique.

Recommended Reading

For those practitioners who are interested in obtaining further information about the principles summarized in this guide the recommended reading list below is provided.

1. Bellman, Geoffrey M., Getting Things Done when You Are Not In Charge, San Francisco, Berrett-Koehler Publishers, 1992.

2. Bennis, Warren, Why Leaders Can't Lead, San Francisco, Jossey-Bass Publishers, 1989.

3. Johnson, Barry, Polarity Management, Identifying And Managing Unsolvable Problems, Amherst, MA, HRD Press, Inc., 1992.

4. Kinlaw, Dennis C., The Practice of Empowerment, Making The Most of Human Competence, London, Gower Publishing Ltd., 1995.

5. Lulic, Margaret A., Who We Could Be At Work, Minneapolis, Blue Edge Publishing, 1994.

6. Morrison, Ann M., The New Leaders, Leadership Diversity in America, San Francisco, Jossey-Bass Publishers, 1996.

7. Quinn, Robert E., Faerman, Sue R., Thompson, Michael P., and McGrath, Michael R., Becoming A Master Manager, New York, John Wiley & Sons, 1990.

8. Smith, Elizabeth A., Creating A Productive Organization, Developing Your Work Force, Manual, St. Lucie Press, Delray Beach, FL, 1995.

9. Tjosvold, Dean and Tjosvold, Mary M., The Emerging Leader, Ways to a Stronger Team, New York, Lexington Books, 1993.

10. Zenger, John H., Musselwhite, Ed., Hurson, Kathleen and Perrin, Craig, Leading Teams, Mastering the New Role, Homewood, Ill., Business One Irwin, 1994.

Test Answers and Skill Dimensions

Below is a list of the leadership skill dimensions that the LST evaluates. The numbers in parenthesis indicate those answers which are most congruent with modern leadership behavior and practices.

Coaching: (02a) (14b) (22b) (40a)

Improving the competencies and commitment of employees through a process of coaching that employs the functions of counseling, mentoring, tutoring and confronting with respect to problems and situations that can affect their job performance.

Communicating: (11b) (26b) (33b) (38b)

Establishing and maintaining open, two-way communication with employees that provides them with essential job related information and obtains feedback about their problems, concerns and suggestions.

Empowering: (06a) (12b) (16a) (20a)

Developing the competencies and influence of employees, both as individuals and as teams of individuals, in a way that involves shared responsibility, shared rewards and a focus on meeting performance objectives.

Facilitating: (25a) (34a) (35b) (37a)

Intervening in the work activities of employees for the purpose of helping them to increase their full performance potential, to solve work related problems and to achieve their performance objectives. Strengthening employees by providing resources, clarifying roles and norms and helping them develop effective work processes.

Influencing: (03a) (09a) (17b) (30b)

Achieving leader acceptance and willing followers by using the process of influence based on the power of expertise and referent power, by inspiring and by creating challenging, achievable goals for employees.

Managing Change: (07a) (10b) (15a) (19b)

Being an effective agent for change by focusing on goal attainment and maintaining a sense of control during periods of uncertainty while at the same time demonstrating flexibility and adaptability. Preparing employees to respond to change in a constructive way.

Managing Projects: (08b) (31b) (36a) (39a)

Envisioning future events and developing strategies for dealing with them. Being able to develop project plans, train and develop project team skills and establish and follow appropriate project control measures to ensure goal attainment.

Servicing Customers: (04b) (13a) (29a) (32b)

Providing quality service to both internal and external customers. Committing oneself and one's team to meeting all of the customer's needs and expectations. Using customer feedback for purposes of continuous improvement.

Solution Finding: (18a) (21b) (23a) (28b)

Defining the problem and understanding the real problem or decision issue. Effectively using both creative and rational problem solving skills in a way that assures full inclusion of all members of the team.

Team Building: (01a) (05a) (24b) (27b)

Accomplishing performance objectives through effective teamwork. Building teams by training employees in team skills, encouraging team interaction and by facilitating team development through open feedback and constructive critique.

Participant Booklet for

LEADERSHIP
SKILLS TEST

by Louis E. Tagliaferri, Ph.D.

MD-127

| DATE: |
| ORGANIZATION: |
| WORK GROUP: |
| NAME: |

LEADERSHIP SKILLS TEST

INSTRUCTIONS: Below are 40 pairs of behaviors and practices that might apply to the role of a leader in any organization. Read each pair of items carefully. Decide which one of each pair you believe is more characteristic than the other of the behavior or practice of a modern leader. Then circle the letter of that item (either "a" or "b") in the column to the left of the pair.

In some cases you may believe that both behaviors or practices in a pair are equally characteristic of a modern leader while in other cases you may believe that neither is characteristic. If the former, select the statement that is most consistent with your beliefs. If the latter, select the statement that is least inconsistent with them.

01. a. Training employees in team skills.

    b. Resolving a conflict between two members of a team.

02. a. Helping employees identify work related problems and causes.

    b. Helping employees cope with problems that adversely affect their quality of life.

03. a. Helping employees solve problems beyond their skill level.

    b. Maintaining control over the tasks and work schedules of employees.

04. a. Analyzing the number and type of customer complaints.

    b. Obtaining feedback from customers about how well their needs were met.

05. a. Meeting with employees in a work unit to discuss how well they work together.

    b. Identify which employees in a group are the potential trouble makers.

06. a. Involving employees in making decisions that affect them.

    b. Ensuring that decisions are made by only the most qualified people.

07. a. Sticking to envisioned objectives even when the unpredicted occurs.

    b. Changing objectives when the unpredicted occurs.

08. a. Beginning the first phase of a project by organizing the necessary resources.

    b. Making sure that the project team is trained in all acquired skills.

09. a. Finding ways to help employees reach their goals and succeed.

    b. Setting realistic goals for your own personal success.

10. a. Asking employees to identify activities that will be hurt by a planned change.

    b. Preparing employees for possible future unplanned changes.

11. a. Checking to see if an employee is following instructions.

    b. Listening to an employee who is complaining about a work assignment.

12. a. Being willing and available to make the necessary decisions.

    b. Authorizing employees to make as many decisions as possible by themselves.

13. a. Knowing who the "customers' are within the organization.

    b. Knowing how the organization's products or services are used.

14. a. Designing a compensation plan that will effectively motivate employees.

    b. Developing an employee's commitment to the process of continual learning.

15. a. Asking for information that will explain the reasons for a planned change.

    b. Offering constructive criticism about planned changes that don't make sense.

16. a. Sharing rewards for success with all members of the team.

    b. Allocating rewards to the most deserving members of the team.

17. a. Having employees solve their own work related problems.

    b. Encouraging employees to discuss their work related problems with you.

18. a. Finding creative solutions to problems.

    b. Making sure that there are no problems.

19. a. Eliminating anything that prevents being able to predict an outcome.

    b. Maintaining a sense of control during periods of uncertainty.

20. a. Making employees understand their responsibility for meeting team goals.

    b. Taking personal responsibility for the team's failure to meet its goals.

21. a. Allocating most of the time to develop a solution to the problem.

    b. Allocating most of the time to identifying the problem and its causes.

22. a. Trying to solve persistent technical problems.

    b. Advising employees about ways to become more sensitive to the organization culture.

23. a. Determining what issues have to be decided in a particular problem.

    b. Determining who caused the problem and why it exists.

24. a. Establishing a relaxed atmosphere to encourage optimum team performance.

    b. Helping work teams stay focused on meeting performance goals.

25. a. Showing employees in a work unit how to critique their team effectiveness.

    b. Establishing controls to maintain work group discipline and morale.

26. a. Explaining work rules to employees.

    b. Keeping employees informed about work related matters that affect them.

27. a. Encouraging friendly competition between the employees of two work groups.

    b. Encouraging employees to work together on a project.

28. a. Deciding which employees have the best skills to solve a work group problem.

    b. Involving all employees in a work group to solve a problem affecting them.

29. a. Responding promptly and effectively to customer complaints.

    b. Developing strategies to deal with difficult customers.

30. a. Developing a fair reward system for ideas and suggestions.

    b. Making sure that employees receive credit for their ideas.

31. a. Using SPC and other statistical methods to develop project schedules.

    b. Developing control methods to ensure that the project plan is followed.

32. a. Producing a product or service of the highest possible quality.

    b. Being committed to meeting all of the customer's expectations.

33. a. Holding a meeting to find out what caused a production problem.

    b. Holding a meeting to obtain employees' suggestions to reduce waste.

34. a. Helping employees find a way to resolve interpersonal conflicts.

    b. Establishing standards for employee conduct and behavior.

35. a. Ensuring that employees arrive at work on time.

    b. Ensuring that employees have the resources they need to do their jobs properly.

36. a. Helping to develop the skills and abilities of project team members.

    b. Replacing unproductive project team members with other employees.

37. a. Helping work teams accomplish their tasks more effectively.

    b. Working on a plan to improve personal time management.

38. a. Completing weekly reports to management about work unit performance.

    b. Ensuring that employees have information they need to do their jobs properly.

39. a. Anticipating future events and planning how to deal with them.

    b. Dealing on a practical level with the problems of today.

40. a. Comparing an employee's actual performance with performance standards.

    b. Deciding what an employee must do to improve job performance.

Management Practices
Inventory II
by
Louis E. Tagliaferri, Ph.D.

Administration Guide
MD-128ELG

Purpose

The purpose of the Management Practices Inventory II (MPI II) is to obtain information about the strengths and development needs of managers, supervisors, and other leaders with respect to essential management and leadership behaviors and practices.

Introduction

The Talico Inc. Management Practices Inventory II (MPI II) is a 360• •developmental assessment and feedback instrument designed to evaluate the behaviors and skills key employees need to lead the work force of the 21st century. The instrument is based on current management and leadership research findings and other literature that identify which work related practices and behaviors must be exercised in the modern work place in order to influence today's employees to achieve their full performance potential. Some of these behaviors and practices are in sharp contrast with the earlier concept that people, like activities or things, can be "managed" in certain rather narrowly prescribed ways in order to achieve optimum efficiency. This latter concept focused on four rather narrowly prescribed functions: planning, organizing, directing and controlling which are also known as the "management cycle." Implicit with that approach was the notion that each of those functions must be managed according to positive human relations precepts.

The "management cycle" functions must still be performed by all managers in essentially any type of organization. Objectives and goals must be established. Strategies that will accomplish goals and objectives must be planned. People, material, technical, financial and other resources must still be gathered and organized and the plan must be implemented. Plan implementation involves staffing, training, coordinating, problem solving and ensuring that the plan is proceeding according to its design and intent and so on. These functions are an integral and essential part of the entire process of successfully operating and managing a business enterprise in any form.

Over the past two decades, however, there has been considerable refinement to the basic "management cycle" based on numerous studies that have identified criteria required for superior organization performance. It has been found, for example, that the most successful leaders and managers not only plan but also have the ability to envision the future in a way that allows them to anticipate and proactively prepare for events yet to occur. We now better understand that leadership is a process of influence rather than power and that effective leaders empower followers through processes like shared responsibility and teamwork. We are also more sensitive to the need for dealing with cultural differentials in the work place, ensuring that one's behavior and conduct conforms with high standards of work ethics, and that change and continuous improvement are inevitable and essential components of the modern work world. The MPI II embodies those refinements and effectively integrates them with the essentials of the indispensable "management cycle" functions.

Description

The MPI II consists of 48 Likert scaled items distributed among the following 12 measurement dimensions.

Leading & Influencing	Managing Change	Coordinating Activities
Communicating	Envisioning	Solving Problems
Building Teamwork	Managing Projects	Ethical Behavior
Managing Diversity	Coaching	Continuous Improvement

MPI II items are in the form of statements which are characteristic of certain executives, managers, supervisors or other leaders. As a 360•·instrument, the MPI II obtains perceptions from up to three organizational levels: self, superior and peer/subordinate. Respondents are asked to decide the extent that each statement is characteristic of the person who is being assessed and whose name appears on the front cover of the instrument (the named person). Response alternatives range from "Very Characteristic" to "Very Uncharacteristic."

The test requires only 15 to 20 minutes to complete. It can be entirely self-administered and self-scored using the manual scoring format in this guide. Optionally, the MPI II can be scored and individual and group profiles can be prepared by the Talico Inc. scoring center. This is an especially helpful option when the test is administered to larger populations. For further information about this option call 904-241-1721.

The product of the test is a profile in the form of a chart that identifies development needs in each skill dimension and that also provides a composite score for the test as a whole. Development needs identification is a function of the multi-level assessment scores that are plotted on skill dimension scales and that are compared with experientially derived training needs thresholds.

Application

The MPI II has many possible applications among employees at any level of the organization. It can be used as a training needs analysis tool for employees who currently hold managerial or supervisory positions or for non-supervisory employees who are candidates for those responsibilities. The MPI II is also ideal for helping to identify employees who have the potential for leadership roles in self-directed work teams, continuous improvement teams or in any other work activity in which an employee must exercise leadership behavior.

Another application for the MPI II is as a learning instrument in a leadership training class. Trainers can use the MPI II to provide feedback to class participants about their management and leadership related beliefs, behaviors and practices. The instrument can also be used as a stand alone performance coaching tool.

Validity

The MPI II was developed by Louis E. Tagliaferri, Ph.D. Dr. Tagliaferri has over 35 years experience as a MD and OD practitioner and is the author of over 100 assessment instruments including the original Management Practices Inventory that was first published in 1977. Content validity for the MPI II was based on identified management and leadership criteria as published in over 150 works including research studies and on data from developmental assessments of more than 1000 managers in business, industry and government. Benchmark management and leadership behaviors and practices were also compared with findings from attitudinal assessments among several thousand employees in both industrial and service industry organizations during the past 5 years. Development needs threshold levels were experientially determined in connection with the above referenced development assessments.

Administration Guidelines

The first step in administering the MPI II is to determine your objectives for using the instrument. There are several ways that it can be used to optimum advantage. Two of the most common usages are for training needs analysis, either individual or group, and for individual performance coaching. Another excellent use is to obtain information that together with other data and information will help you identify individuals with managerial or leadership potential. Still another use is as a learning instrument that can be integrated with a training course about management practices and leadership.

In all cases remember that the MPI II is a multi-level assessment instrument. Another common term for this type of instrument is a "360•ᵛ inventory. Both terms refer to the fact that in order to obtain optimum value from the instrument one copy must be completed by people in each of three organizational levels: the person who is being assessed, that person's supervisor and either subordinates or peers of the assessed person. The scoring of the MPI II is based on its design usage as a three (3) level assessment instrument. If you administer it to only the assessed person or to just one other level (but not to all three levels) then the scores that you derive from the activity cannot accurately be related to the threshold scores in the scoring guide.

Whether you administer the MPI II to only a few individuals or to a group it is very important to ensure that participants clearly understand the instrument's purpose and objectives and how you intend to use the MPI II scores. You should inform test participants that the MPI II has been designed as a developmental tool, to help identify training and development needs for employees who either are currently in a leadership role or who are candidates for a leadership role. You should explain that the scores are an index of how they are perceived to exercise the various skills, functions and behaviors that comprise the items in the inventory. Because total job performance is a function of many different factors -- not just the factors measured by the MPI II -- you should emphasize that the MPI II results for any individual is not the same as a complete performance appraisal for that individual; although the MPI results can be used to supplement the latter. The point is that you should stress development -- not evaluation.

It is not practicable to discuss all of the possible MPI II administration scenarios in this guide. However, the following suggestions are based on the most way that most organizations have successfully administered the MPI II. Naturally, you should adapt these steps to the particular circumstances within your organization.

1. Establish specific objectives for using the MPI II. Decide exactly what you want to accomplish by using the instrument and how you intend to use the results. Note: while it is not absolutely essential that you feedback MPI II results to the individuals who are assessed, it is **highly** recommended that you do so.

2. Select the population to be assessed. Each of these individuals must complete one copy of the MPI II.

3. Select the individuals who will participate in the exercise by completing one copy each of the MPI II for an individual assessed person. The assessed person's supervisor is an essential party to this exercise. Then, you must determine whether subordinate or peers of the assessed person will participate as well. We strongly recommend that you have at least four other people (in addition to the supervisor and the assessed person) complete the MPI II for each assessed person. More than four is even better. In order to ensure rating objectivity select these people at random. Do not select only those people who you believe will likely rate the assessed person favorably or unfavorably.

4. A few days before the assessment exercise send a letter to all participants in which you explain the exercise purpose, objectives, general method and in which you state how the results will be used. Many organization hold brief meetings of all involved in the exercise for this purpose.

5. Obviously the ratings of the assessed person (called the "named person in the actual questionnaire) and that person's supervisor will be identified with the rater. However, because four or more "others" will be selected to assess rate the assessed person the anonymity of these latter people can and should be maintained. All they need to do is to indicate that they are either subordinates or peers of the "named person." The assessed person's supervisor and all of the "others" will require one copy each of the MPI II>

6. At the time of the exercise distribute one copy of the MPI II to each person participating in the exercise. It is recommended that you provide confidential return envelopes so that each respondent can send his/her completed MPI II to a designated person, like a training or other HRD person. If you decided to administer the MPI II in group meetings (a good option) be sure to proctor the session. Then collect the MPI IIS from all respondents after they have completed the form. In the latter case you may choose to read the instructions aloud to the group and then to answer any questions they may have before they begin to complete the inventory.

7.	After you have receive the competed MPI IIS score them using the scoring instructions and scoring guides in this manual. You may photocopy the two **MPI II Scoring Guide** templates so that you have one set for each assessed person. If you have administered the MPI II to a large population you may want to set up a simple spreadsheet in your computer to facilitate scoring the larger numbers of inventories. Alternatively, Talico Inc. offers a scoring service. Call 904-241-1721 for further information about this service.

8.	When scoring has been completed you are ready to begin using MPI II results. Whether your purpose for the exercise concerned training or coaching we recommend that one copy of the MPI II Scoring Guide for an assessed person be given to both the individual and to his/her supervisor. A meeting should be scheduled between the two parties with the objective that they should focus on both the assessed person's scores for each measurement dimension and also on the variance between the ratings of the three levels. It will be helpful if a photocopy of the MPI II Categories & Items that is included in this guide is provided to both parties for reference purposes. Item numbers in the MPI II Scoring Guides correspond with the item numbers in the former.

	Significant variances in perceptions about how characteristic each MPI II behavior item is of the assessed person may be caused by lack of clarity in performance standards or job responsibilities, poor performance related communication or other causes which could adversely affect job performance if left unresolved.

9.	Following the feedback meeting and discussion, the assessed person should complete a personal development plan. A self-guided model for such a plan is included in this guide and may be photocopied for each assessed person.

10.	Follow up is an essential part of any developmental action plan. In addition to follow up action between the assessed person and his/her supervisor, we suggest that a remeasure again using the MPI II take place approximately 12 months after the first exercise. This will enable all parties to determine what progress has been made against objectives for improvement.

As stated earlier, results from the MPI II can be used for training needs analysis purposes. Training professionals who are involved in such activities should develop group profiles by simply averaging MPI II scores for individuals into composite set scores. This will identify skill dimensions in which the group needs the greatest training and development.

MPI II Personal Developmental Plan

Prepare a development plan to improve your management and leadership practices by answering the questions below. Be sure to set specific development objectives with time lines.

A. The management and leadership practices that are currently my greatest strengths are:

_____
_____
_____
_____

B. The management and leadership practices which I need to strengthen most are:

_____
_____
_____
_____

C. My personal objectives for improving my management and leadership practices are:

_____
_____
_____
_____

D. The specific strategies by which I plan to develop and strengthen my management and leadership practices are (use additional paper if necessary):

1. _____
_____
_____

2. _____
_____
_____

3. _____
_____
_____

4. _____
_____
_____

Recommended Reading

For those practitioners who are interested in obtaining further information about the principles summarized in this guide the recommended reading list below is provided.

1. Bellman, Geoffrey M., *Getting Things Done when You Are Not In Charge,* San Francisco, Berrett-Koehler Publishers, 1992.

2. Bennis, Warren, *Why Leaders Can't Lead,* San Francisco, Jossey-Bass Publishers, 1989.

3. Dubois, David D., *Competency-Based Performance Improvement: A Strategy for Organizational Change,* Amherst, MA, HRD Press, 1993.

3. Johnson, Barry, *Polarity Management, Identifying And Managing Unsolvable Problems,* Amherst, MA, HRD Press, Inc., 1992.

4. Kinlaw, Dennis C., *The Practice of Empowerment, Making The Most of Human Competence,* London, Gower Publishing Ltd., 1995.

5. Lulic, Margaret A., *Who We Could Be At Work,* Minneapolis, Blue Edge Publishing, 1994.

6. Morrison, Ann M., *The New Leaders, Leadership Diversity in America,* San Francisco, Jossey-Bass Publishers, 1996.

7. Quinn, Robert E., Faerman, Sue R., Thompson, Michael P., and McGrath, Michael R., *Becoming A Master Manager,* New York, John Wiley & Sons, 1990.

8. Smith, Elizabeth A., *Creating A Productive Organization, Developing Your Work Force, Manual,* St. Lucie Press, Delray Beach, FL, 1995.

9. Tjosvold, Dean and Tjosvold, Mary M., *The Emerging Leader, Ways to a Stronger Team,* New York, Lexington Books, 1993.

10. Tjosvold, Dean and Tjosvold, Mary M., *Leading The Team Organization,* New York, Lexington Books, 1991.

10. Zenger, John H., Musselwhite, Ed., Hurson, Kathleen and Perrin, Craig, *Leading Teams, Mastering the New Role,* Homewood, Ill., Business One Irwin, 1994.

MPI II Categories & Items

Building Teamwork

01. Emphasize the importance of team performance more than individual performance?
02. Involve all work unit employees in making decisions and solving problems that affect the team?
03. Help a work unit grow and develop by candidly evaluating its own performance as a team?
04. Help the team stay focused on achieving its performance goals?

Coaching

05. Confront employees about problems that they may be having with their job performance?
06. Conduct meaningful one-on-one meetings with an employee to identify the cause of a performance problem that he/she may be having?
07. Establish specific performance goals for or with employees?
08. Help employees develop insight into the causes and possible solutions of any job related problems that they may be having?

Communicating

09. Share job related information openly and candidly with employees?
10. Encourage ideas and suggestions from others?
11. Listen carefully to understand the message or point of view of others?
12. Respond to what others are saying in a way that encourages further communication?

Continuous Improvement

13. Continuously seek ways to improve work methods or procedures?
14. Encourage employees to be creative and innovative?
15. Focus on achieving total quality results?
16. Ensure that employees receive continuous education and training to improve their job skills?

Coordinating Activities

17. Effectively coordinate work activities among employees in his/her work unit?
18. Empower employees through the process of shared responsibility?
19. Maintain good work relationships with peers in other departments?
20. Ensure that the activities of his/her work unit are properly coordinated with related activities in other work units?

Envisioning

21. Accurately anticipate future events that may affect his/her work unit?
22. "See the whole picture" rather than just the part that he/she may play in a project or work activity?
23. Set goals for his/her work unit that are supportive of the broader goals of the whole organization?
24. Develop strategies that will effectively deal with anticipated future opportunities or problems?

Ethical Behavior

25. Demonstrate proper respect for the dignities and sensitivities of others?
26. Perform his/her job in a way that fully conforms with all ethical codes and practices of the business or profession?
27. Complies with all relevant laws and statutes relating to the performance of his/her responsibilities?
28. Performs his/her job in a diligent and competent manner?

Leading & Influencing

29. Successfully represent the interests of employees to higher organizational levels?
30. Demonstrate a high degree of job knowledge and competency?
31. Integrate the needs of work unit members with the mission and objectives of the organization?
32. Adapt his/her style of leadership to deal with the circumstances of the specific task and people involved?

Managing Change

33. Feel comfortable dealing with change such as in work methods or procedures?
34. Remain focused on envisioned objectives when the unpredictable occurs?
35. Help employees prepare for future change?
36. See change as an opportunity for improvement rather than as a barrier or impediment?

Managing Diversity

37. Demonstrate that he/she is personally committed to getting involved with employees of other cultural backgrounds?
38. Demonstrate awareness about the needs and concerns of culturally diverse employees?
39. Train employees in ways to make decisions that are fair to culturally diverse employees?
40. Recognize and resolve discrimination against employees of culturally diverse backgrounds?

Managing Projects

41. Develop effective strategies to accomplish project goals and objectives?
42. Organize human, material, technical and other resources so that a project plan can be properly implemented?
43. Ensure that the project staff has the required skills and other competencies perform their assignments?
44. Establish controls to ensure that the project proceeds according to plan?

Solving Problems

45. Accurately identify the real problem or decision issue?
46. Gather all relevant facts about the decision issue or problem before acting?
47. Demonstrate skill in team problem solving techniques?
48. Use valid, rational methods to solve problems or make decisions?

APPENDIX A   **How To Score It**

The MPI II provides you with two types of training needs information. It gives you scores for each training needs analysis set. Within each set, it shows you the relative assessments of the three organizational levels rating the manager or supervisor. The MPI II SCORING GUIDE on pages X and Y of this guide is used to record all of this data.

The MPI II can easily be scored by following these steps.

1. Plot the individual item ratings of the manager or supervisor (SELF) and his or her (SUPERIOR) in each set grid as appropriate. Identify the different ratings with symbols such as • = SELF, x = SUPERIOR.

2. Average the SUBORDINATES/PEERS' scores for each MPI II item and plot the averages in each set grid using the symbol o = SUBORDINATES.

3. Total the MPI II item scores for each level within each set and record the sum for the appropriate rating level in the space to the right of each grid.

4. Total the SELF, SUPERIOR and SUB/PEERS scores to arrive at a set score.

5. Set scores of 40 or lower and single item MPI II totals (the total of the ratings of all three levels for one item) of 10 or lower indicate that the manager or supervisor would likely benefit from additional training.

6. Be sure to carefully study the single item totals to identify any significant perceptual differences among the rating levels. Significant perceptual differences could indicate other problems such as frequent misunderstandings, unclear role/responsibility definition, etc.

EXAMPLE

The MPI II point values are:

Very Characteristic = 5
Characteristic = 4
Somewhat Characteristic = 3
Uncharacteristic = 2
Very Uncharacteristic = 1

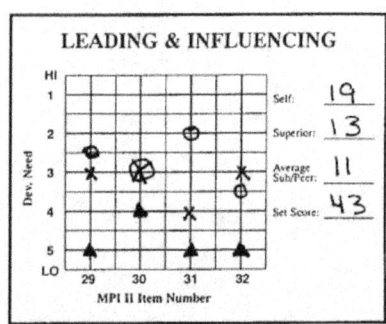

70

MPI II Scoring Guide

BUILDING TEAMWORK

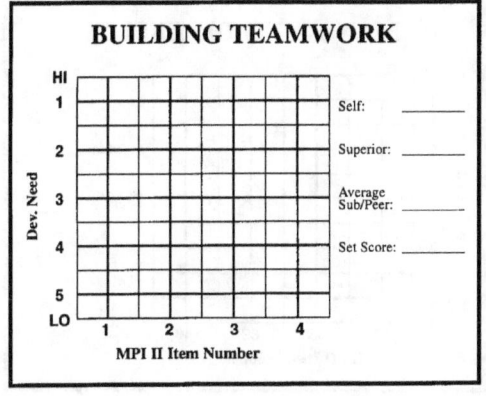

Dev. Need — HI 1 2 3 4 5 LO
MPI II Item Number: 1 2 3 4

Self: _____
Superior: _____
Average Sub/Peer: _____
Set Score: _____

CONTINUOUS IMPROVEMENT

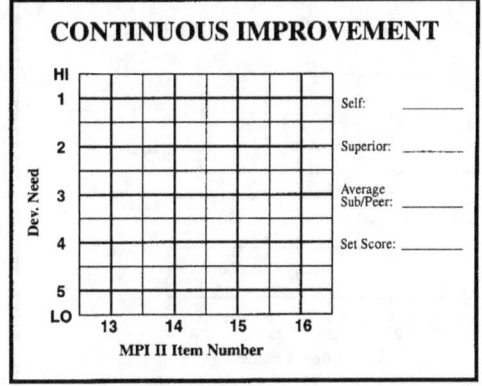

Dev. Need — HI 1 2 3 4 5 LO
MPI II Item Number: 13 14 15 16

Self: _____
Superior: _____
Average Sub/Peer: _____
Set Score: _____

COACHING

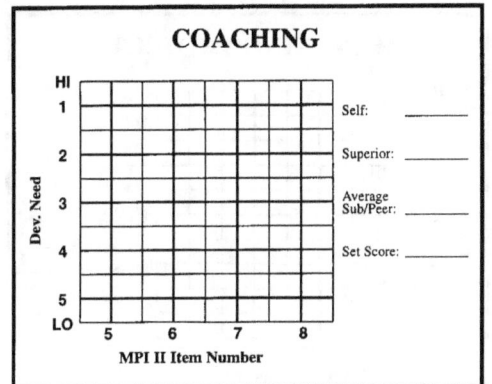

Dev. Need — HI 1 2 3 4 5 LO
MPI II Item Number: 5 6 7 8

Self: _____
Superior: _____
Average Sub/Peer: _____
Set Score: _____

COORDINATING

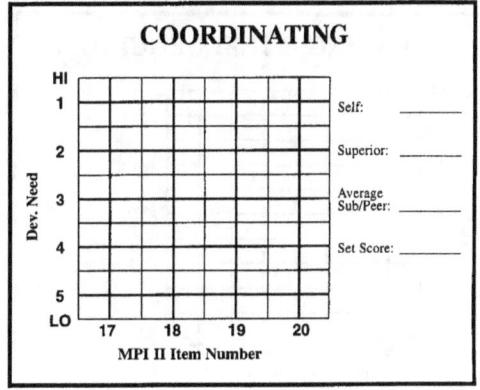

Dev. Need — HI 1 2 3 4 5 LO
MPI II Item Number: 17 18 19 20

Self: _____
Superior: _____
Average Sub/Peer: _____
Set Score: _____

COMMUNICATING

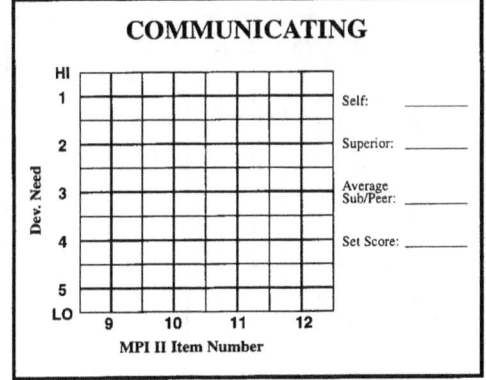

Dev. Need — HI 1 2 3 4 5 LO
MPI II Item Number: 9 10 11 12

Self: _____
Superior: _____
Average Sub/Peer: _____
Set Score: _____

ENVISIONING

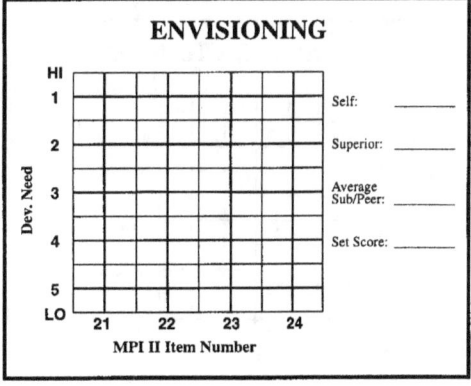

Dev. Need — HI 1 2 3 4 5 LO
MPI II Item Number: 21 22 23 24

Self: _____
Superior: _____
Average Sub/Peer: _____
Set Score: _____

MPI II Scoring Guide

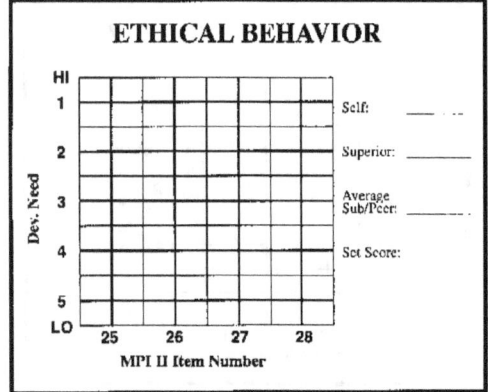

ETHICAL BEHAVIOR

Dev. Need — HI 1, 2, 3, 4, 5 LO

MPI II Item Number: 25 26 27 28

Self: _____
Superior: _____
Average Sub/Peer: _____
Set Score: _____

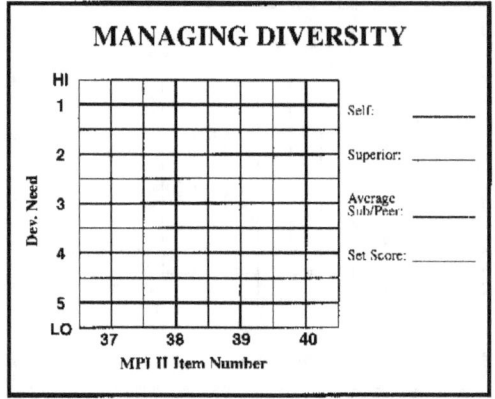

MANAGING DIVERSITY

Dev. Need — HI 1, 2, 3, 4, 5 LO

MPI II Item Number: 37 38 39 40

Self: _____
Superior: _____
Average Sub/Peer: _____
Set Score: _____

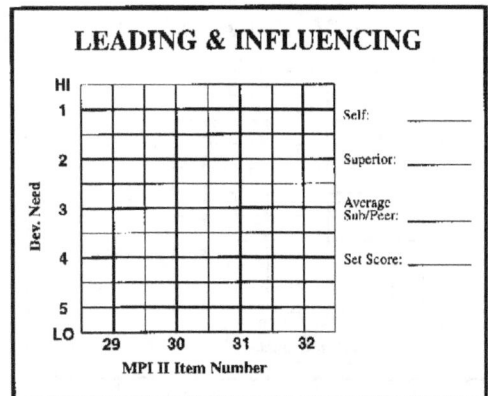

LEADING & INFLUENCING

Dev. Need — HI 1, 2, 3, 4, 5 LO

MPI II Item Number: 29 30 31 32

Self: _____
Superior: _____
Average Sub/Peer: _____
Set Score: _____

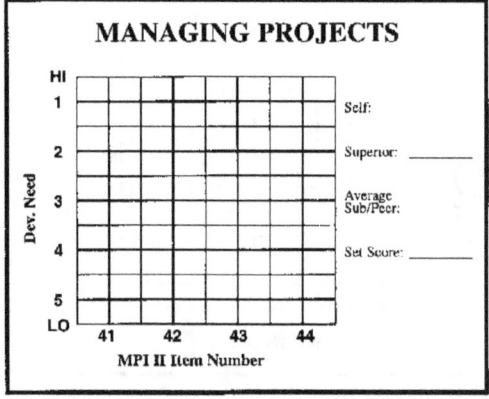

MANAGING PROJECTS

Dev. Need — HI 1, 2, 3, 4, 5 LO

MPI II Item Number: 41 42 43 44

Self: _____
Superior: _____
Average Sub/Peer: _____
Set Score: _____

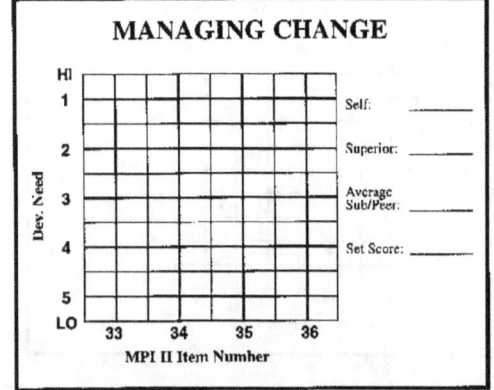

MANAGING CHANGE

Dev. Need — HI 1, 2, 3, 4, 5 LO

MPI II Item Number: 33 34 35 36

Self: _____
Superior: _____
Average Sub/Peer: _____
Set Score: _____

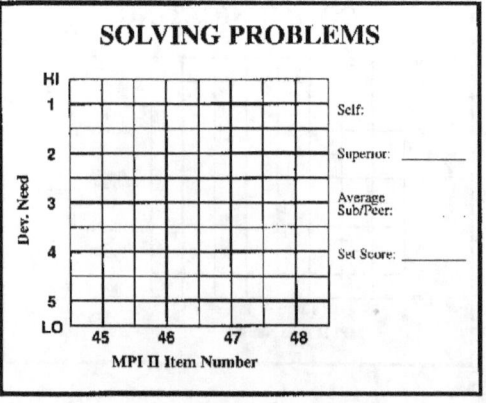

SOLVING PROBLEMS

Dev. Need — HI 1, 2, 3, 4, 5 LO

MPI II Item Number: 45 46 47 48

Self: _____
Superior: _____
Average Sub/Peer: _____
Set Score: _____

Participant Booklet for

MANAGEMENT PRACTICES INVENTORY II

by Louis E. Tagliaferri, Ph.D.

MD-128

MANAGEMENT PRACTICES INVENTORY II

INSTRUCTIONS

The purpose of this inventory is to obtain your opinion about how characteristic the following 48 statements are regarding the person whose name appears on the front cover (the "named person"). You may be that person himself or herself, a subordinate, associate or peer of that person or that person's supervisor. Please read each statement carefully. Then indicate how characteristic you believe each statement is of the person and mark your choice in the appropriate column to the right of the statements. Thank you.

EXAMPLE:

	Very Characteristic	Characteristic	Somewhat Characteristic	Uncharacteristic	Very Uncharacteristic
51. Coordinates projects with other employees.	❑	❑	❑	❑	❑

By selecting the alternative "Somewhat Characteristic" you would have indicated that in your opinion it is Somewhat Characteristic for the named person to coordinate projects with other employees.

Before you begin your assessment, please turn to the front cover and identify your role in relation to the named person. Do not provide your name if you are a peer, associate or subordinate of the named person. Thank you for your help in this important exercise.

How characteristic is it for the named person to:	Very Characteristic	Characteristic	Somewhat Characteristic	Uncharacteristic	Very Uncharacteristic
01. Emphasize the importance of team performance more than individual performance?	❑	❑	❑	❑	❑
02. Involve all work unit employees in making decisions and solving problems that affect the team?	❑	❑	❑	❑	❑
03. Help a work unit grow and develop by candidly evaluating its own performance as a team?	❑	❑	❑	❑	❑
04. Help the team stay focused on achieving its performance goals?	❑	❑	❑	❑	❑
05. Confront employees about problems that they may be having with their job performance?	❑	❑	❑	❑	❑
06. Conduct meaningful one-on-one meetings with an employee to identify the cause of a performance problem that he/she may be having?	❑	❑	❑	❑	❑
07. Establish specific performance goals for or with employees?	❑	❑	❑	❑	❑
08. Help employees develop insight into the causes and possible solutions of any job related problems that they may be having?	❑	❑	❑	❑	❑
09. Share job related information openly and candidly with employees?	❑	❑	❑	❑	❑

	Very Characteristic	Characteristic	Somewhat Characteristic	Uncharacteristic	Very Uncharacteristic
10. Encourage ideas and suggestions from others?	❑	❑	❑	❑	❑
11. Listen carefully to understand the message or point of view of others?	❑	❑	❑	❑	❑
12. Respond to what others are saying in a way that encourages further communication?	❑	❑	❑	❑	❑
13. Continuously seek ways to improve work methods or procedures?	❑	❑	❑	❑	❑
14. Encourage employees to be creative and innovative?	❑	❑	❑	❑	❑
15. Focus on achieving total quality results?	❑	❑	❑	❑	❑
16. Ensure that employees receive continuous education and training to improve their job skills?	❑	❑	❑	❑	❑
17. Effectively coordinate work activities among employees in his/ her work unit?	❑	❑	❑	❑	❑
18. Empower employees through the process of shared responsibility?	❑	❑	❑	❑	❑
19. Maintain good work relationships with peers in other departments?	❑	❑	❑	❑	❑
20. Ensure that the activities of his/her work unit are properly coordinated with related activities in other work units?	❑	❑	❑	❑	❑
21. Accurately anticipate future events that may affect his/her work unit?	❑	❑	❑	❑	❑
22. "See the whole picture" rather than just the part that he/she may play in a project or work activity?	❑	❑	❑	❑	❑
23. Set goals for his/her work unit that are supportive of the broader goals of the whole organization?	❑	❑	❑	❑	❑
24. Develop strategies that will effectively deal with anticipated future opportunities or problems?	❑	❑	❑	❑	❑
25. Demonstrate proper respect for the dignities and sensitivities of others?	❑	❑	❑	❑	❑
26. Perform his/her job in a way that fully conforms with all ethical codes and practices of the business or profession?	❑	❑	❑	❑	❑
27. Complies with all relevant laws and statutes relating to the performance of his/her responsibilities?	❑	❑	❑	❑	❑
28. Performs his/her job in a diligent and competent manner?	❑	❑	❑	❑	❑
29. Successfully represent the interests of employees to higher organizational levels?	❑	❑	❑	❑	❑
30. Demonstrate a high degree of job knowledge and competency?	❑	❑	❑	❑	❑

	Very Characteristic	Characteristic	Somewhat Characteristic	Uncharacteristic	Very Uncharacteristic
31. Integrate the needs of work unit members with the mission and objectives of the organization?	❑	❑	❑	❑	❑
32. Adapt his/her style of leadership to deal with the circumstances of the specific task and people involved?	❑	❑	❑	❑	❑
33. Feel comfortable dealing with change such as in work methods or procedures?	❑	❑	❑	❑	❑
34. Remain focused on envisioned objectives when the unpredictable occurs?	❑	❑	❑	❑	❑
35. Help employees prepare for future change?	❑	❑	❑	❑	❑
36. See change as an opportunity for improvement rather than as a barrier or impediment?	❑	❑	❑	❑	❑
37. Demonstrate that he/she is personally committed to getting involved with employees of other cultural backgrounds?	❑	❑	❑	❑	❑
38. Demonstrate awareness about the needs and concerns of culturally diverse employees?	❑	❑	❑	❑	❑
39. Train employees in ways to make decisions that are fair to culturally diverse employees?	❑	❑	❑	❑	❑
40. Recognize and resolve discrimination against employees of culturally diverse backgrounds?	❑	❑	❑	❑	❑
41. Develop effective strategies to accomplish project goals and objectives?	❑	❑	❑	❑	❑
42. Organize human, material, technical and other resources so that a project plan can be properly implemented?	❑	❑	❑	❑	❑
43. Ensure that the project staff has the required skills and other competencies to perform their assignments?	❑	❑	❑	❑	❑
44. Establish controls to ensure that the project proceeds according to plan?	❑	❑	❑	❑	❑
45. Accurately identify the real problem or decision issue?	❑	❑	❑	❑	❑
46. Gather all relevant facts about the decision issue or problem before acting?	❑	❑	❑	❑	❑
47. Demonstrate skill in team problem solving techniques?	❑	❑	❑	❑	❑
48. Use valid, rational methods to solve problems or make decisions?	❑	❑	❑	❑	❑

Management Training
Needs Analysis

by
Louis E. Tagliaferri, Ph.D.

Administration Guide
MD-108ELG

WHAT IT IS

The Management Training Needs Analysis (MTNA) is a 48 item, multi-level instrument that identifies training needs among managers and supervisors. It covers twelve skill dimensions that are essential to successful managerial and supervisory performance. Skill dimensions are:

- LEADERSHIP
- TRAINING
- HUMAN RELATIONS
- MOTIVATION
- COMMUNICATION
- DISCIPLINE & CONTROL
- PERFORMANCE MGT.
- PROBLEM SOLVING
- PLANNING & ORGANIZING
- WORK ASSIGNMENTS
- TIME MANAGEMENT
- COUNSELING

The MTNA measures perceptions from three organizational levels (self, superior and subordinates) regarding the amount of training that a manager or supervisor needs tin order to perform his/her job effectively.

WHO IT IS FOR

The MTNA will produce the best results when it is used to assess training needs among first-line through mid-level managers and supervisors.

HOW IT WAS DESIGNED

The design and construction of the MTNA is based on the concept and principles embodied in the well-known "management cycle" and "supervisory process". The test focuses on the critical practices and behaviors which are identified in both concepts. Recognizing that the technical skills required of a manager or supervisor will vary considerably from job to job. the MTNA concentrates on identifying training needs primarily in the areas of human interaction and conceptual skills.

The instrument design ensures proper universe of content, simplicity of item wording, and a minimum of acquiescence and social desirability bias. Reliability is assured in that each variable is measured by two or more items. The scale construction is one that has proven to be accurate and easy-to-use.

HOW TO SCORE IT

The MTNA provides you with two types of training needs information. It gives you scores for each training needs analysis set. Within each set, it shows you the rela-

tive assessments o the three organizational levels rating the manager or supervisor. The reproducible MTNA scoring grids on pages 3 and 4 of this guide are used to record all of this data.

The MTNA can easily be scored as follow:

1. Plot the individual item ratings of the manager or supervisor (SELF) and his or her (SUPERVISOR) in each set grid as appropriate. Identify the different ratings with symbols such as ▲ = self, x = SUPERIOR.

2. Average the SUBORDINATES/PEERS' scores for each MTNA item and plot the averages in each set grid using the symbol o = SUBORDINATES.

3. Total the MTNA item scores for each level within each set and record the sum for the appropriate rating level in the space to the right of each grid.

4. Total the SELF, SUPERIOR and SUB/PEERS scores to arrive at a set score.

5. Set scores of 40 or lower and single item MTNA totals (the total of the ratings of all three levels for one item) of 10 or lower indicate that the manager or supervisor would likely benefit from additional training.

6. Be sure to carefully study the single item totals to identify any significant perceptual differences among the rating levels. Significant perceptual differences could indicate other problems such as frequent misunderstandings, unclear role/responsibility definition, etc.

EXAMPLES

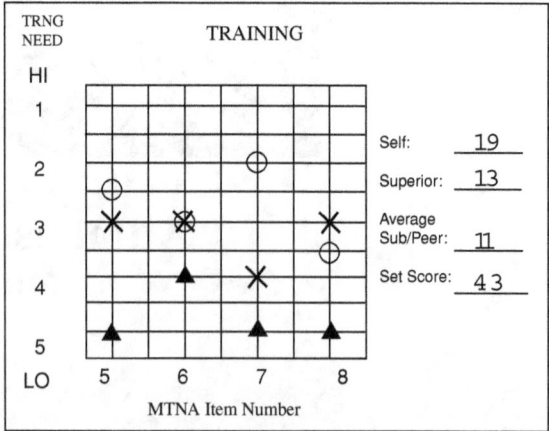

MTNA Scoring Guide

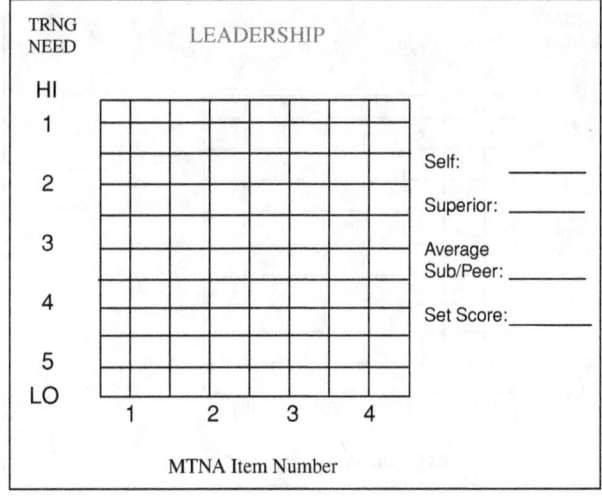

LEADERSHIP

TRNG NEED

HI
1
2
3
4
5
LO

1   2   3   4

MTNA Item Number

Self: _____
Superior: _____
Average Sub/Peer: _____
Set Score: _____

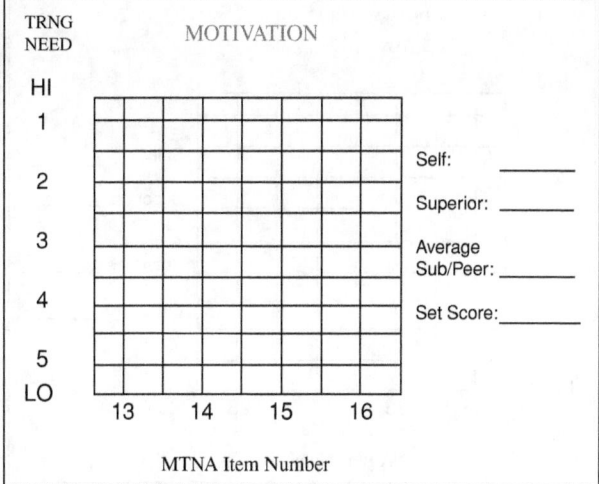

MOTIVATION

TRNG NEED

HI
1
2
3
4
5
LO

13   14   15   16

MTNA Item Number

Self: _____
Superior: _____
Average Sub/Peer: _____
Set Score: _____

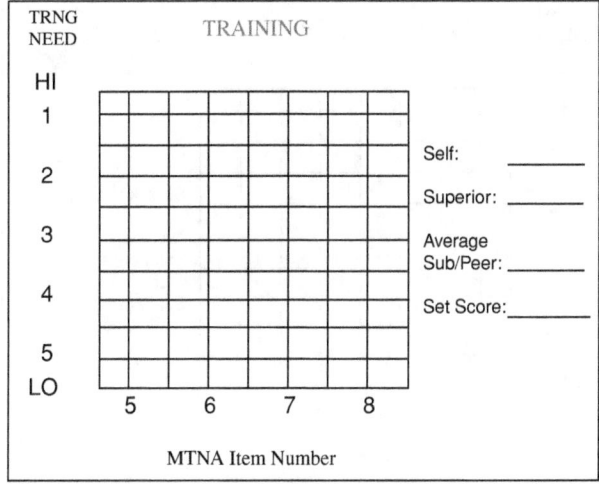

TRAINING

TRNG NEED

HI
1
2
3
4
5
LO

5   6   7   8

MTNA Item Number

Self: _____
Superior: _____
Average Sub/Peer: _____
Set Score: _____

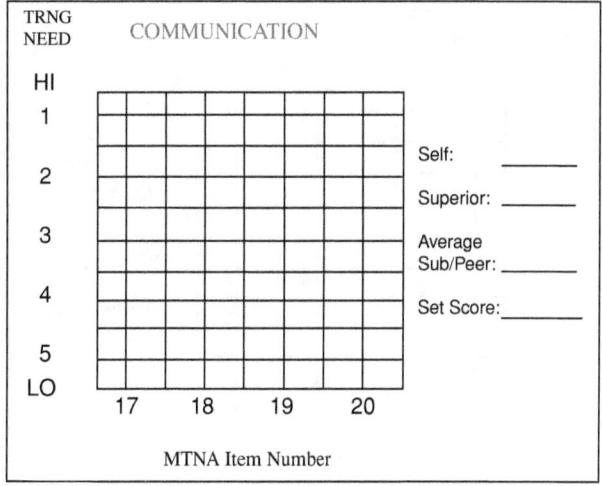

COMMUNICATION

TRNG NEED

HI
1
2
3
4
5
LO

17   18   19   20

MTNA Item Number

Self: _____
Superior: _____
Average Sub/Peer: _____
Set Score: _____

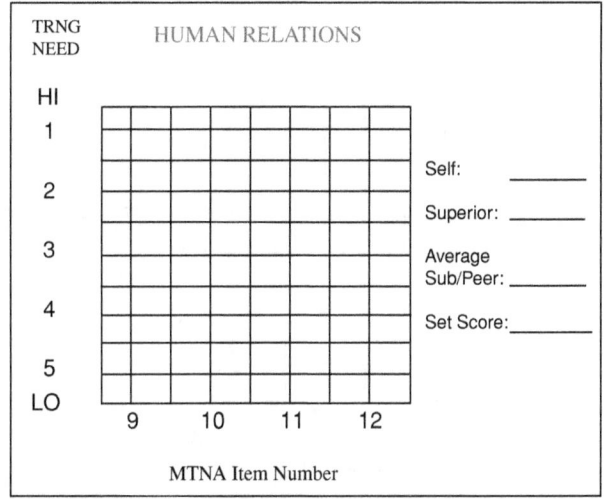

HUMAN RELATIONS

TRNG NEED

HI
1
2
3
4
5
LO

9   10   11   12

MTNA Item Number

Self: _____
Superior: _____
Average Sub/Peer: _____
Set Score: _____

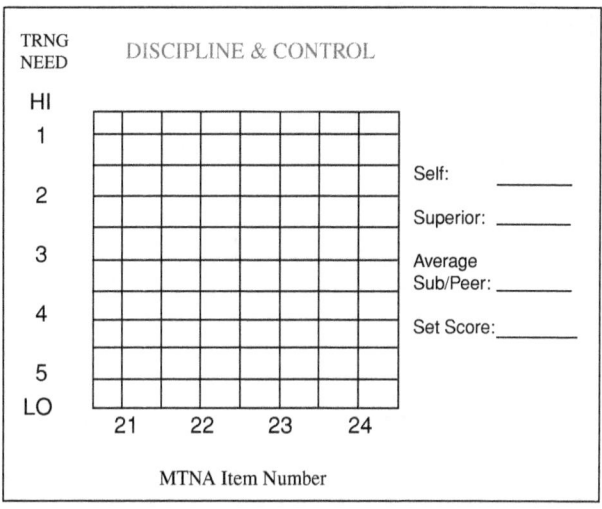

DISCIPLINE & CONTROL

TRNG NEED

HI
1
2
3
4
5
LO

21   22   23   24

MTNA Item Number

Self: _____
Superior: _____
Average Sub/Peer: _____
Set Score: _____

MTNA Scoring Guide

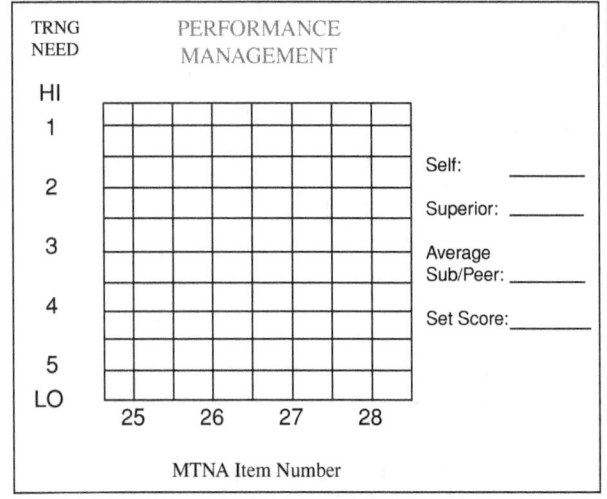

TRNG NEED

PERFORMANCE MANAGEMENT

HI
1
2
3
4
5
LO

25 26 27 28

MTNA Item Number

Self: _____
Superior: _____
Average Sub/Peer: _____
Set Score: _____

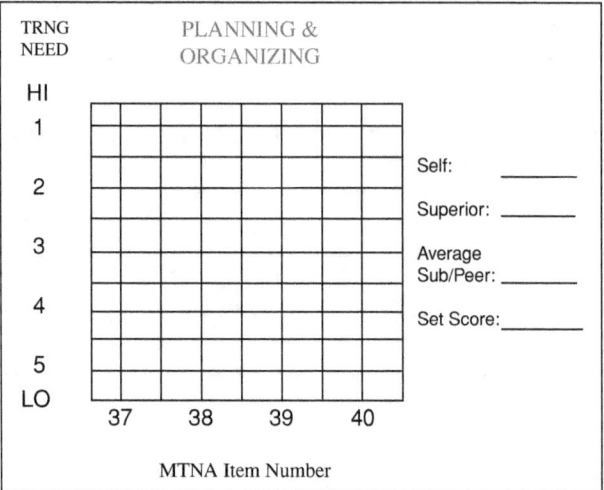

TRNG NEED

PLANNING & ORGANIZING

HI
1
2
3
4
5
LO

37 38 39 40

MTNA Item Number

Self: _____
Superior: _____
Average Sub/Peer: _____
Set Score: _____

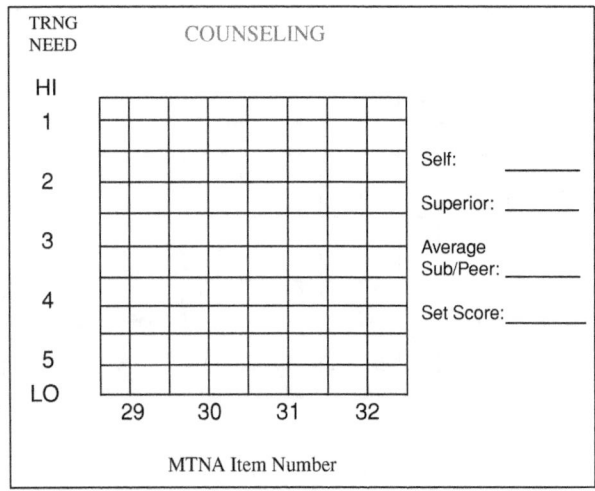

TRNG NEED

COUNSELING

HI
1
2
3
4
5
LO

29 30 31 32

MTNA Item Number

Self: _____
Superior: _____
Average Sub/Peer: _____
Set Score: _____

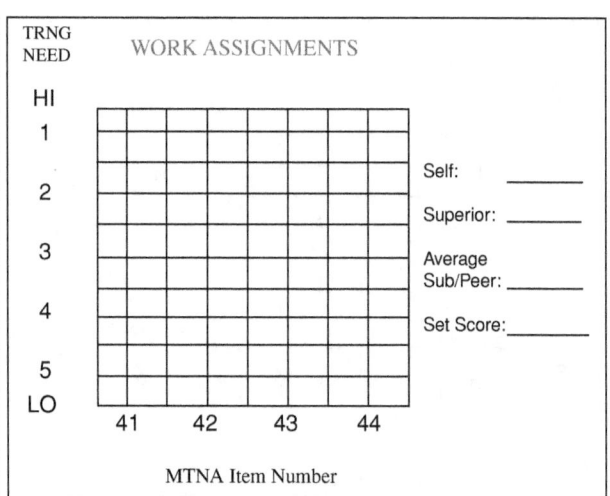

TRNG NEED

WORK ASSIGNMENTS

HI
1
2
3
4
5
LO

41 42 43 44

MTNA Item Number

Self: _____
Superior: _____
Average Sub/Peer: _____
Set Score: _____

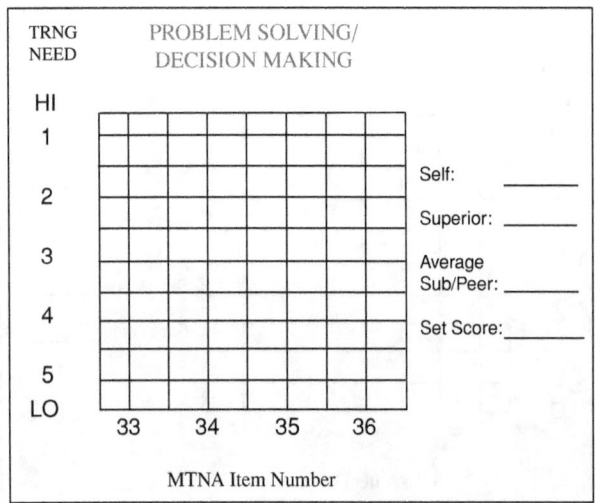

TRNG NEED

PROBLEM SOLVING/ DECISION MAKING

HI
1
2
3
4
5
LO

33 34 35 36

MTNA Item Number

Self: _____
Superior: _____
Average Sub/Peer: _____
Set Score: _____

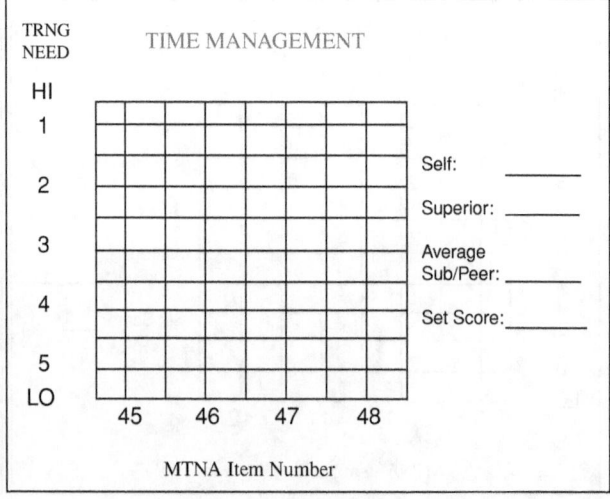

TRNG NEED

TIME MANAGEMENT

HI
1
2
3
4
5
LO

45 46 47 48

MTNA Item Number

Self: _____
Superior: _____
Average Sub/Peer: _____
Set Score: _____

Participant Booklet for

MANAGEMENT TRAINING NEEDS ANALYSIS

by Louis E. Tagliaferri, Ph.D.

MD-108

| ORGANIZATION: |
| ASSESSMENT OF: |
| YOU ARE: |
| ❏ The above person
❏ The superior of the above person
❏ A peer/subordinate of the above person |

INSTRUCTIONS

The purpose of this questionnaire is to obtain your opinion about the amount of additional training that the person whose name appears on the front cover needs in order to be as effective as possible in his or her job. Below are 48 behaviors or practices that are common to the jobs of many managers and supervisors. Read each item carefully. Then circle the number on the scale to the right of each item that most closely corresponds with your assessment of the amount of additional training that the named person needs.

MANAGERIAL WORK BEHAVIORS AND PRACTICES

		Very Considerable	Considerable	Some	Little	Very Little
01.	Maintaining good relationships with subordinates.	1	2	3	4	5
02.	Directing the efforts of subordinates toward a common goal.	1	2	3	4	5
03.	Determining which leadership approach is best for a particular situation.	1	2	3	4	5
04.	Modifying leadership style as the situation requires.	1	2	3	4	5
05.	Instructing new employees in proper job methods.	1	2	3	4	5
06.	Training employees in new or revised job methods.	1	2	3	4	5
07.	Checking progress of trainees.	1	2	3	4	5
08.	Using effective training methods and techniques.	1	2	3	4	5
09.	Dealing with subordinates in a fair, consistent and uniform manner.	1	2	3	4	5
10.	Understanding the emotions, attitudes and beliefs that can affect employee behavior.	1	2	3	4	5
11.	Dealing with difficult personalties.	1	2	3	4	5
12.	Involving subordinates in decision making.	1	2	3	4	5
13.	Giving recognition to subordinates who do a good job.	1	2	3	4	5
14.	Motivating the average employee.	1	2	3	4	5
15.	Understanding what motivates employees.	1	2	3	4	5
16.	Enriching the quality of subordinates' work life.	1	2	3	4	5
17.	Communicating with subordinates openly and honestly.	1	2	3	4	5
18.	Encouraging candid feedback from subordinates.	1	2	3	4	5

MANAGERIAL BEHAVIORS AND PRACTICES

	Very Considerable	Considerable	Some	Little	Very Little
19. Keeping superiors informed about job related matters.	1	2	3	4	5
20. Coordinating activities with peers in other departments.	1	2	3	4	5
21. Understanding all of the organization's personnel policies, practices and procedures.	1	2	3	4	5
22. Using progressive discipline.	1	2	3	4	5
23. Administering discipline when needed.	1	2	3	4	5
24. Ensuring that discipline is administered in a fair, uniform and consistent manner.	1	2	3	4	5
25. Informing subordinates about job standards and expectations.	1	2	3	4	5
26. Providing subordinates with timely, accurate feedback about their job performance.	1	2	3	4	5
27. Taking effective corrective action to improve employee work performance.	1	2	3	4	5
28. Maintaining effective controls over costs and quality.	1	2	3	4	5
29. Listening to employees' complaints and problems.	1	2	3	4	5
30. Counseling subordinates about job related problems or complaints.	1	2	3	4	5
31. Having empathy for subordinates' concerns or needs.	1	2	3	4	5
32. Following up on employees' complaints.	1	2	3	4	5
33. Identifying what the real problem or issue is.	1	2	3	4	5
34. Determining problem root causes.	1	2	3	4	5
35. Using effective problem solving methods.	1	2	3	4	5
36. Using group decision making techniques.	1	2	3	4	5
37. Setting precise, measurable and realistic goals.	1	2	3	4	5
38. Developing plans or strategies to accomplish objectives.	1	2	3	4	5
39. Organizing staff, material or other resources.	1	2	3	4	5
40. Establishing clear lines of authority and responsibility.	1	2	3	4	5

MANAGERIAL BEHAVIORS AND PRACTICES

		Very Considerable	Considerable	Some	Little	Very Little
41.	Making clear, understandable work assignments.	1	2	3	4	5
42.	Delegating work to subordinates when appropriate.	1	2	3	4	5
43.	Ensuring that the right person is assigned to the job.	1	2	3	4	5
44.	Following up to ensure that work assignments are properly carried out.	1	2	3	4	5
45.	Effectively planning and scheduling subordinates' work activities.	1	2	3	4	5
46.	Effectively planning and scheduling own work activities.	1	2	3	4	5
47.	Prioritizing project and other work activities.	1	2	3	4	5
48.	Meeting assigned schedules and deadlines.	1	2	3	4	5

PLEASE ANSWER THE FOLLOWING QUESTIONS

1. What are the most significant strengths of the named person?

2. What are the most urgent developmental needs of the named person?

3. Additional comments:

Supervisory
Skills Builder

by
Louis E. Tagliaferri, Ph.D.

Facilitators Guide
MD-131LG

Synopsis

Title: Supervisory Skills Builder

Time: About 1½ hours

Objective: To improve the understanding of supervisory employees or candidates for supervisory positions about key principles of supervisory leadership.

Description: This is a learning instrument. As such it can be used as an instructional aid as well as an assessment instrument. In Part I of the instrument there are 60 true/false Pre-Test items allocated among six measurement dimensions:

T-1   Communication
T-2   Coaching & Counseling
T-3   Employee Motivation
T-4   Empowerment
T-5   Leadership
T-6   Team Building

The purpose of the Pre-Test is to establish a baseline measurement for the test respondent. Part II consists of brief notes that summarize the key supervisory skills principle relevant to each test item. Then, in Part III respondents take a Post-Test that consists of the same 60 items in the Pre-Test. After completion of the Post-Test the respondent can compare his or her Pre-Test baseline score with the Post-Test score and calculate gain scores or improvement. The Post-Test results will also help the respondent pinpoint skill dimensions and specific skill issues that might require further reinforcement.

Method: This is a binary response scale instrument designed to be completed by individuals in a self-study, pre-class mode

Material: One copy of the Facilitator's Guide for the facilitator and one copy of the Supervisory Skills Builder booklet for each test respondent.

Application: Basic supervisory skills development or as a refresher for employees who have participated in earlier supervisory skills training programs.

Suitable for: This instrument is suitable for candidates for supervisory positions, first-line supervisors and mid-level supervisors.

Presentation Guidelines

The purpose of this section is to give you a set of guidelines that will help you to administer the Supervisory Skills Builder as effectively as possible. As in the case of all instructional presentations, preparation is one of the major keys to success. An important premise is that you, as facilitator and presenter, are sufficiently knowledgeable about the skill dimensions in this instrument that you can answer any questions that the respondents might have about the individual test items and/or the key notes for each item.

1. Use the masters that are included on the CD-ROM for this product to reproduce as many copies of the Supervisory Skills Builder as you will require.

2. Distribute one copy of the test booklet to each test respondent. For your convenience, a copy of the test booklet is reproduced in this guide as it appears to the respondent.

3. Begin by explaining the purpose of the instrument and the specific learning objectives that you have set for the individual or group. Present a brief overview of the instrument including an explanation about how the test results and content instruction will be used.

4. Read the introduction and instructions of the instrument aloud to the respondent(s). Inform the respondent(s) that they must complete all three parts of the instrument before you will provide them with the scoring key. Ask them to refrain from referring to Part II when completing the two tests. Answer any questions that they might have about the instrument or its relevancy to their jobs.

5. Tell the respond(s) that there is no time limit for the test but that they should be able to complete it in less than one and one-half hours.

6. After the respondent(s) has completed the Supervisory Skills Builder provide them with a copy of the scoring key in Appendix A to this guide. Instruct the respondent(s) to score the instrument and to record the scores to Part I in the Pre-Test Baseline Score box and the scores to Part III in the Post-Test Score Box. Urge the respondent(s) to restudy any supervisory skills principle that they still do not fully understand after completing the Post-Test.

7. If you choose to base a training module on the Supervisory Skills Builder be sure to instruct test respondents to bring their copy of the completed instrument with them to class. The content structure of Part II of the instrument will serve as an excellent base for you to conduct a guided discussion of supervisory skills principles.

Supervisory Skills Builder

by
Louis E. Tagliaferri, Ph.D.

Respondent Booklet
MD-131EPB

Welcome to Supervisory Skills Builder, a short self-instruction learning instrument that will familiarize you with key interaction skills that are necessary for effective supervisory leadership.

There are three parts to this instrument. In Part I you will be given a pre-test that consists of 60 true-false items, each measuring an important key principle of supervisory leadership. Read each test item and indicate whether you believe that it is true or false. When you have completed the test you will calculate a base line score. The purpose of this part of the program is to help you assess the current level of your knowledge about supervisory leadership interaction skills.

Part II of the program consists of 6 sections, each representing a key skill dimension:

    T-1 Communication
    T-2 Coaching & Counseling
    T-3 Employee Motivation
    T-4 Empowerment
    T-5 Leadership
    T-6 Team Building

In this part of the program ten key principles of each of the above skill dimensions will be presented. Be sure to read each of these principles carefully. Each numbered principle corresponds with a test item of the same number. The purpose of this part of the program is to familiarize you with each supervisory leadership principle and its rationale.

Lastly, Part III is a retest of the principles which you studied in Part II. After completing the test in Part III you can then compare your final test results with your base line score in Part I to determine the extent to which you have improved your understanding of supervisory leadership skill principles. If your final test score indicates that you would benefit by reviewing the learned principles you can "jump" back to Part II and restudy those principles in which you still need reinforcement.

Part I Pre-Test

T-1 Communication

T   F

☐   ☐   1. The primary communication responsibility of supervisors is to pass important job related information downward to employees.

☐   ☐   2. The most effective form of communication is a carefully worded memo or letter.

☐   ☐   3. The listening effectiveness of the average person is only about 25%.

☐   ☐   4.   Active listening is a term that describes a three step process for improving listening effectiveness.

☐   ☐   5. The "grapevine" is a useful and effective channel of communication in almost any organization.

☐   ☐   6. In order to improve work unit communication, supervisors should make a point of talking with employees about matters of legitimate interest to them such as company policy, work methods, sports, political, or religious matters.

☐   ☐   7. Much of the message content exchanged between people ion a face-to-face conversation is nonverbal in nature.

☐   ☐   8. Higher management should be the primary source of authoritative job-related information for employees in most organizations.

☐   ☐   9. One sign of an effective communication process is the absence or near absence of complaints or grievances.

☐   ☐   10. The single most important human interaction skill for a supervisor is the skill of effective listening.

T-1 Nr. Correct: _____

T-2 Coaching & Counseling

T   F

☐   ☐   11. In many cases what an employee complains about is not really what is bothering them.

☐   ☐   12. Formal complaint or problem solving procedures should be avoided because they tend to limit a supervisor's ability to resolve issues that bother employees.

☐   ☐   13. In most cases supervisors lack the authority to resolve an employee's problem or complaint.

☐   ☐   14. Counseling employees about problems or complaints requires well developed listening skills.

☐   ☐   15. Because "off-the-job" personal problems can affect an employee's performance at work, supervisors should always be willing to discuss these non-job related problems with them.

☐   ☐   16. Coaching and counseling are the same thing.

☐   ☐   17. In most cases supervisors should avoid being critical of an employee's job performance because employees generally resent being told that they are doing something wrong.

☐   ☐   18. Coaching includes confronting an employee about job performance problems.

☐   ☐   19. For the convenience of both the employee and the supervisor work related problems or complaints should be discussed promptly after they occur and at the employee's work station.

☐   ☐   20. It is more difficult to change an employee's attitude or work behavior than it is to increase their job knowledge and skills.

T-2 Nr. Correct: _____

T-3 Employee Motivation

T   F

☐   ☐   21. Motivation is based on a person's needs or goals.

☐   ☐   22. Once an important need has been fulfilled it no longer serves as a strong motivator.

☐   ☐   23. Recognition is most effective when it is administered as soon as possible after a task is performed well.

☐   ☐   24. Whether or not a supervisor is able to use motivation effectively or not depends largely on the nature of the job.

☐   ☐   25. Employees who perform routine, repetitive, and monotonous tasks are usually less productive than those whose jobs are more fulfilling.

☐   ☐   26. Administering discipline to an employee usually tends to lower work group motivation.

☐   ☐   27. Studies show that pay is actually a potential dissatisfier -- not a true motivator.

☐   ☐   28. Higher management is usually in a better position than the immediate supervisor to motivate employees.

☐   ☐   29. In order for a reward to motivate an employee not only must it be important but the employee must also believe that it is attainable.

☐   ☐   30. Motivation is the act of getting people to want to perform a task willingly and effectively.

T-3 Nr. Correct: _____

T-4 Empowerment

T   F

☐   ☐   31. Empowerment is based on the concept of shared responsibility.

☐   ☐   32. Empowerment as a work practice can be used in most organizations anytime, under almost any circumstance.

☐   ☐   33. In order for empowerment to exist all members of a work team must take part in making all of the decisions affecting the team.

☐   ☐   34. Empowerment is more effective when the nature of the work to be done is highly structured rather than creative and open-ended.

☐   ☐   35. One of the weaknesses of the empowerment concept is that the role of a leader becomes so unclear that management control can be lost.

☐   ☐   36. Before an empowerment program can be successfully implemented there must be a high degree of trust and mutual respect between management and employees.

☐   ☐   37. In order to optimize performance, supervisors of empowered work units should encourage friendly competition among their employees.

☐   ☐   38. Empowered employees should be involved with setting their own performance goals but not with developing strategies for accomplishing departmental goals.

☐   ☐   39. Empowerment does not work effectively when applied to culturally diverse groups of employees.

☐   ☐   40. There are no formally appointed leaders in an empowered work force.

T-4 Nr. Correct: _____

T-5 Leadership

T   F

☐   ☐   41. Leadership can be defined as the act of getting things done through others.

☐   ☐   42. A leader cannot lead unless followers accept and follow his or her leadership.

☐   ☐   43. Most successful leaders rely on the power of their appointed position to get things done.

☐   ☐   44. The most effective leaders select a leadership style that suits them and use it consistently in any situation they encounter.

☐   ☐   45. The most important focus of leadership is on people and on maintaining positive human relationships.

☐   ☐   46. Employee involvement in decision making frees the leader from responsibility for the results of the decision.

☐   ☐   47. A supervisor has only one major responsibility -- to get the job done according to standards set by his or her employer.

☐   ☐   48. When confronted with difficult situations like having an employee balk at accepting a less desirable work assignment, supervisors should take advantage of any past social or personal relationships in order to get the job done without a hassle.

☐   ☐   49. Good leaders are born -- not made.

☐   ☐   50. In order to maintain their personal credibility supervisors should candidly tell employees about any organization policy or higher management decisions with which they (the supervisor) disagree.

T-5 Nr. Correct: _____

T-6 Team Building

T   F

☐   ☐   51. In a work place a team is any informal group of employees who share a common interest.

☐   ☐   52. Teamwork cannot exist unless employees are formed into formal teams.

☐   ☐   53. There are two essential sets of functions that any effective team must perform, interpersonal relationship functions and task performance functions.

☐   ☐   54. Conflict among members of a team is usually destructive and should be avoided if possible or suppressed if it does arise.

☐   ☐   55. The primary strategy of team building is to increase the awareness of team members about their own process as a team.

☐   ☐   56. A major problem with being part of a team is that individual accomplishments are no longer recognized.

☐   ☐   57. Team loyalty requires that team members pull together to defend members against criticism by using techniques such as explaining, justifying and rationalizing.

☐   ☐   58. Encouraging constructive competition between individuals in the same work unit will almost always help to foster a team spirit.

☐   ☐   59. Team leaders should focus on building employee commitment rather than on building performance controls.

☐   ☐   60. Team problem solving is usually a slower process than problem solving by competent individual contributors who may be working either as a member of the team or independent of the team.

T-6 Nr. Correct: _____

Pre-Test Baseline Score	
Skill Area	No. Correct
T-1	
T-2	
T-3	
T-4	
T-5	
T-6	
TOTAL	

Part II Key Supervisory Principles

T1 - Communication

1. Communication can be defined as the sharing and understanding of information among people. In a work environment this means that there must be a full and complete sharing of job related information, especially among people who work together. Supervisors have an especially important communication role. True, they must provide job related information to employees like work instructions, organization policy, procedures, etc. "downward" to employees. But, they must also obtain feedback communication from employees about job related problems, concerns, suggestions for improvement and much more. Further, supervisors must obtain and share job related information with their superiors and with people in other work units. The primary communication responsibility of supervisors, therefore is much broader than just downward communication.

2. The most effective form of communication takes place when two or more people are in direct face-to-face contact sharing information in a multi-media way. This means that they share verbal communication, obtain verbal and non-verbal feedback from each other, show, illustrate and explain and, if appropriate, use other communication aids such as audio-visual aids. Written communication is among the least effective means of sharing information. It is one-way and does not allow immediate feedback.

3. Some years ago an experiment was conducted at Ohio State University to determine how well people really listen to what someone else is saying. The results showed that about 75% of what one person said to another was lost in transit. The researchers were astounded at the results and re-conducted the study. However, once again the results were clear. Most people simply are poor listeners. They allow listening barriers like preconceptions, anticipating what the other person is going to say, disagreement with what the other person is saying and many other similar barriers to adversely affect their listening effectiveness. The good news is that the same studies showed that with even a little training listening effectiveness can be significantly improved.

4. There are three components in the process that is called active listening. The first is to listen to what the other person is saying with the intent to understand and without raising barriers like objections, anticipation, interruptions and so on. The second component is to acknowledge to the other person that you do hear and understand their point of view, even if you disagree with it. A nod of the head or a comment like "I see" or "I understand what you are saying" illustrate this component. Lastly, active listening also involves responding to the other person in a way that encourages them to continue speaking and to continue sharing information. Examples of this would be to say something like "Could you explain why you feel that way further?" or "I'd like to understand your feelings about that better."

5. The term "grapevine" as it is used in the context of organizational communication has long referred to informal communication like passing rumors from one person to another. Today it would also be synonymous with the term "leak" such as information being "leaked" to the

press. In any of its many forms information passed along the "grapevine" is very often inaccurate, incomplete or misleading. While the "grapevine" can probably never be eliminated, no one should rely on information from that source.

6. Supervisors should make a point of establishing good two-way communications with all of their employees. However, it is almost never appropriate to engage in a conversation with employees about their political, or religious beliefs or practices. This does not mean that the only permitted communication between a supervisor and his or her subordinates (or with others, for that matter) is strictly job related. There are obvious appropriate non-work related subjects that can be brought into a conversation between them, like sports, weather, certain social events, and other "safe" subjects. But, there are lines that should almost never be crossed and two of them are to discuss an employees political or religious beliefs.

7. Body language, nonverbal communication, has been found to convey as much as 60% or more of a message's true content. Looks, facial expressions, body stances, spacing between the people who are communicating, gestures and other nonverbal signals are essential to effectively getting a message accurately conveyed to another person when in face-to-face communication. If you doubt this then the next time that you are communicating with someone face-to-face watch for any body language signals that they send in response to what you are saying and be sensitive about the body language signals that you are sending to the other person.

8. In essentially any organization the primary source of timely, accurate and authoritative information for employees should be their immediate supervisor. It is the immediate supervisor who has the major day-to-day contact with the employee and who is the critical link between the employee and higher management. Important job related information that is obtained by employees from other sources than their supervisor often tends to weaken the supervisor's leadership role as perceived by the employees. That is one reason why following the "chain of command" is important.

9. It is a healthy sign when employees feel comfortable speaking up to express their concerns, problems or complaints. Concerns, problems or complaints will exist whether or not employees bring them up to their supervisors. When they do not feel comfortable doing so it is often because they feel intimidated by the supervisor or they feel that the supervisor does not care about these matters or that the supervisor is powerless to do anything about them. All supervisors should strive to achieve a situation where employees feel free to come to them with these matters and with their suggestions for improvement anytime.

10. Over the years many studies have been conducted among employees to find out what attributes are most important to them on the part of their supervisor. Consistently, these studies can be summed up by what one employee said: "I like my job, my supervisor listens to me."

T2 - Coaching and Counseling

11. It is very important that supervisors not only be willing to listen and respond to employee complaints but also have the skill to identify the real problem issue. Often what an employee complains about is not really the problem. For example, an employee might complain about their job not paying enough but in reality the issue may be that they believe that they are not being treated the same as other employees i.e. that there is an inequity with respect to pay for employees who are doing the same type of work. Complaints can help supervisors understand the hidden attitudes and feelings of employees. But, in order to accomplish this supervisors must not only must practice active listening but also must be able to distinguish between the symptom of a problem and the problem root cause.

12. In most organizations a formal complaint or problem solving procedure is essential in order to maintain a positive human relations atmosphere. Indeed, in most unionized organizations a formal grievance procedure is an inevitable part of the labor agreement. While it is preferred that the majority of employee problems and complaints be resolved at the lowest possible level, especially at the level of the complainant and his or her immediate supervisor, realistically not all will be resolved that way. If there is no formal process for employees to refer unresolved problems or complaints to higher authority (after attempts to resolve them with their immediate supervisor have failed) then those problems and complaints will remain, fester and ultimately negatively impact quality, productivity and other performance elements.

13. Most job related problems or complaints that employees have concern their immediate work environment, the elements of their job, or the interpretation and application of organization policies and work rules by their immediate supervisor. Because of this it is exactly the immediate supervisor who is in the best position to counsel employees about these matters and to resolve them.

14. It was earlier stated that the most important human interaction skill that a supervisor can have is the skill of effective listening. Counseling employees about their problems or complaints is one of the most common examples of situations where this skill is absolutely essential. Often there is a great deal of emotionality on the part of an employee who is having a job related problem or who is making a complaint. Supervisors who are counseling employees, especially under these circumstances, must be able to objectively listen to and understand what the employee is really saying or trying to say, put the employee at ease by acknowledging understanding and encourage the employee to offer as much information as possible that will lead to a practicable problem resolution.

15. The only off-the-job problems that a supervisor should discuss with an employee are those that directly affect their job. For example, suppose that an employee is being counseled about an unacceptable attendance record and raises a child care issue as an excuse. Obviously, that personal problem directly impacts the employee's job performance and can be included as a discussion issue in the counseling session. On the other hand, if there is no job relatedness, such as being related to a job performance situation, an employee's marital problem is not an appropriate subject for discussion. And, even if the employee were to state

that the marital problem is affecting his or her job performance the supervisor is not the person who in most cases is qualified to discuss it. In such an event, and other similar cases, the supervisor should seek guidance from his or her superior and or the organization's human resource specialists.

16. Coaching and counseling are both interaction skills. In a work environment they both involve a supervisor or someone else in a leadership role, or even a staff specialist, interacting with an employee, usually through discussion, about a job related matter of interest or concern to either or both parties. Both require effective listening skills on the part of the coach or counselor and both require other effective communication skills such as the skill of indirect questioning. However, the focus of the interaction in coaching is quite different from that in counseling. The focus in coaching is on job performance; the qualitative or quantitative aspects of the job with respect to identifying and overcoming performance deficiencies or coaching for the purpose of further improving already satisfactory job performance. The focus of counseling could be to simply discuss a complaint that an employee has or to explain how an employee can qualify for a certain benefit such as a medical or retirement benefit.

17. Coaching employees about job performance problems, especially when unsatisfactory performance is involved, is a key responsibility of all supervisors. Further, industrial studies have shown that most employees want to know when they are not meeting job expectations and what they can do to improve their performance in order to meet job standards. Supervisors should remember that in order for employees to perform at their best they must clearly understand what the job standards are, how well they are meeting those standards, and what can be done to meet them, if there are deficiencies, or to exceed them if performance is already satisfactory.

18. The focus of coaching is on job performance. When there are no performance deficiencies then coaching can deal with ways to further improve an employee's job performance -- much like a sports coach continuously tries to "coach" an athlete to better his or her performance. When there are job performance problems then coaching must confront the employees with them, identify the causes of the problems and develop remedial strategies.

19. Work related problems and complaints are matters personal to the employee and should be discussed in private. The exceptions would be situations when a supervisor must demonstrate how an employee should perform a task correctly at his or her work station, safety issues that are occurring at the work station and must be immediately corrected or similar urgent issues which cannot be discussed elsewhere.

20. Knowledge can be increased fairly easily by reading a book, taking a self-instruction training course such as this, or by other instruction. Skill development requires practice. For example, one cannot become a good golfer just by reading a book about golf. When a person's attitude is set it requires a great deal of logic and persuasion to change it. Even then many people will simply not modify their behavior. If you doubt this think about dieting!

T3 - Employee Motivation

21. Perhaps because it has such an impact not only on our personal lives but also within the work environment the subject of motivation has been extensively researched. The essence of motivation is an inner desire to make an effort. What has intrigued researchers is what stimulates that desire. Today it is generally accepted that motivation is based on a person's needs or goals and that there is a ranking or hierarchy of human needs which motivate all of us. As it applies to the work environment the most basic need is to obtain and hold a job of sufficient nature that it will provide the income necessary for our support and that of our families. But, there are other job related needs as well. For example, the need for affiliation with other employees, a certain degree of job status, and eventually the satisfying nature of the job itself with the prospect of being able to be fulfilled in one's work -- self actualization. The idea is that our desire to make an effort is a function of how much we need or want these things.

22. If a person is very thirsty he or she will be motivated to seek out water or something else to quench his or her thirst. But, after that thirst is quenched it no longer serves as a motivator -- until the next time. A person is motivated to pursue a certain career goal, perhaps a promotion. The promotion is obtained and for a while satisfies the person. But, as time passes most people would begin thinking of even further advancement and thus the first job to which they aspired, and now hold, no longer offers the same challenge so they are motivated to seek something else, possibly even a career change.

23. Suppose you did an especially good job in a project but your boss waited 6 months, for no good reason, to say "oh, by the way, that was a fine job you did 6 months ago." How would you feel? You would probably say to yourself "Yeah, great. What took you so long to tell me?" In contrast, if the boss came up to you right after the job, when you were feeling especially good about it anyway because you knew that you did well, and complimented you then the recognition would have meant so much more.

24. The nature of the job is itself a motivator, of course. However, even when a job is boring, routine or underutilizes a person's skills the supervisor can still recognize things such as excellent performance, consistent good quality, positive job attitude, or many other things.

25. Many highly structured jobs that require little more than "tending" by employees enable the employee to be highly productive due to technology. At the same time, it is entirely possible that the same job is dissatisfying to the employee and because of this serves as a demotivator. Supervisors should understand that although having a highly motivated work force is very important there are other factors, like technology, that can affect productivity.

26. Employees expect that supervisors will take corrective action with nonperformers or with employees who violate work rules. If disciplinary action is not taken when warranted then the result can be demotivating to the other employees in the work group.

27. Job related attributes like pay, benefits, status and the more physical aspects of a job are important. But, studies have shown that while you can be sure that employees will be dissatisfied if they are not present at competitive levels, their existence does not ensure satisfaction. One major company gave a 10% pay increase to all employees and later studies its motivational effect. The results showed that the motivational value of that increase lasted 19 days. After that employees were figuratively saying "Yes, that was good but what has the company done for me lately?" On the other hand, what has been found to be true satisfiers or motivators are attributes like the job itself, opportunities for growth and advancement, responsibility and recognition.

28. By now you should clearly understand the importance of the role of the immediate supervisor. It is an employee's immediate supervisor, for better or worse, who has the greatest impact on the level of motivation of the employee -- not higher management which is often far removed from direct contact with the employee.

29. There is a string of three criteria that determine whether or not a reward (recognition, a promotion, more responsibility or even a pay increase) will motivate an employee, even for a short while like pay does. First, the reward must have importance to the employee. It must satisfy a need or a goal. Secondly, the employee must feel that he or she is capable of perform the job task associated with the reward. If the person lacks the requisite training, for example, then the person might believe that there is no use trying to do the job because he or she does not know how to do it. Lastly, the employee must believe that if task performance is successful the reward will in fact be given to him or her. In other words, it must be attainable.

30. This relates to the principle that motivation is an inner desire to make an effort. Remember, people can be forced to do a job but that is not really motivation. Under those circumstances they may perform the job at the minimum level necessary to "get by." That does not contribute to the level of quality performance that most organizations need to be competitive in today's market place.

T4 - Empowerment

31. Perhaps the first thing that should be understood about empowerment is that it is not entirely new. It is simply a new term that has been given to a "Quality of Work Life" process that began in the era pf post-World War II when industry began focusing more seriously on the human factor in the work place. One example of this movement was the emphasis given to participative management in the 1960s through the present time; a process of involving employees in making decisions that affect them at work. Empowerment goes one step further. It means that power or authority, responsibility, communication, decisions and rewards for accomplishments are shared among employees and management.

32. Empowerment is actually very difficult, costly and time consuming practice. It is one thing for managers and supervisors to accept the concept that employees should have a say in matters affecting them. But it is less easy for managers, supervisors, and even for employees to accept and effectively implement the idea that some important responsibilities and decisions formerly the exclusive prerogative of management should now be vested in the hands of employees; decisions, perhaps, like product design, production methods, quality standards, even staffing decisions. In most organizations this requires a cultural change together with extensive training for managers and employees.

33. The key is to involve those who should be involved, but not necessarily all of the employees all of the time. It is not necessary that all employees be involved in making all of a work group's decisions all of the time. If that were the case then business would grind to a halt every time a decision had to be made.

34. Empowerment can work in operations where the job tasks are highly proceduralized and it can work in operations like research laboratories where the work is very unstructured. There are likely greater opportunities for empowerment, however, in work environments where the job tasks require more judgement on the part of the employees. Less opportunity for decision making discretion is available to employees on a highly robotized auto assembly line, for example, than in a bank, insurance company or in a sales organization.

35. Leadership is exercised in a different way in an empowered work environment but management control, in the sense of responsibility for the final product of work effort, is neither lost nor abdicated to the employees. In an empowered work organization the role of leader is more that of coach and facilitator rather than that of a director of work activities. Supervisors and other leaders help employees accomplish mutually agreed work objectives and serve as helpful troubleshooters when things do not go as planned.

36. This is one reason why empowerment cannot work successfully everywhere. In many organizations there is neither the job nor psychological maturity among either management or employees that is required for implementation of a successful empowerment program. For example, management must have done its part to ensure a highly skilled, well trained work force. That enables management to have confidence in employees' judgement, ideas and suggestions. In turn, employees must believe that management will be truly responsive to their suggestions for cost, quality and productivity improvement and that if those suggestions improve profitability management will share the rewards with them. Of course, there are many other factors as well.

37. There is a popular misconception that competition among employees usually improves performance. Indeed, it is easy to cite examples where at least for a limited period of time competition did just that, either among individuals or among entire work teams. However, research has conclusively shown that on a long term basis cooperation and collaboration -- teamwork -- will be more effective. This is not limited just to empowered work groups but it is true throughout business, industry and government.

38. They should be involved in both sets of activities. That is one of the major points of having an empowered work force. It is the realization and acceptance that responsible, well trained employees have an incredible amount of talent that can be tapped to help improve overall organization performance. This principle was understood several decades ago when participative management was introduced and when Japanese Quality Circles found their way to the United States and elsewhere.

39. Empowerment in culturally diverse work places is often more easily implemented and is more successful than in other types of organizations. One reason for this is that the North American work culture has until fairly recently placed more emphasis on competition than on teamwork. However, in many parts of Asia, Europe and other regions of the world the individual has always been subordinate to the group. Thus, the concept of working together collaboratively for many culturally diverse employees is quite natural.

40. It is true that self-directed work teams are very common in organizations where empowerment has been adopted. However, in most cases there are still managers, supervisors, team leaders, administrators and other formally appointed leaders by whatever title. The distinction is that leadership in empowered work environments is through coaching, facilitating, supporting and helping rather than by the exercise of traditional control techniques.

T5 - Leadership

41. In reality almost everyone of us is a leader or has been one at sometime in our lives. This is because leadership is accomplished through the power of influence. Whenever we influence others, in any way or in any manner (positive or negative) to do something that we want done then we have exercised leadership, we got something done through others. Naturally there is a lot more to leadership than just getting somebody to do something. How one got somebody to do something, what style of leadership they used, the effectiveness of their leadership and many other factors come into play as we learn more about this interesting subject. However, in essence the definition is quite simple - getting things done through others.

42. We all have the ability to either accept or refuse to accept the leadership role of another person, whether or not they have been appointed to a position of authority over us. The price of refusing to obey a leader may be quite steep. In a work environment the person who refuses to obey a lawfully given order would be guilty of insubordination and likely disciplined. But, the employee had the choice to follow the instruction or, if he or she felt strongly enough about the issue, refuse to obey and accept the consequences. In the latter case the leader, no matter how coercive he or she might have been, had no power to lead if the employee chose not to accept his or her leadership. There are many degrees of acceptance of leadership on the part of employees and in reality this is the norm. It is one thing to accept and follow a leader's instructions yet another to do so with enthusiasm. The effective leader is one who can influence people so that they willingly and freely accept his or her leadership role.

43. There are several ways that leaders can influence people so that they can get things done. One is appointed position power, a traditional role in that most people simply accept that a boss has the right to tell them what to do. Other leaders lead through the power of charisma letting their dynamic personality influence others. Many people are able to lead, influence others, by the power of their expertise. For example, most people readily follow the advice of their physicians or attorneys. In business there are many examples of people with certain technical expertise essentially leading others with less expertise in the subject. Some people still try to lead by using reward and punishment. But, there is a growing trend in today's work place for leaders to use the power of rational agreement to influence others. This is best illustrated in situations where organizations place a lot of emphasis on teamwork, work force participation in decision making and where the work culture supports empowerment.

44. Studies have clearly shown that there is no one best way to lead all of the people in all situations that might arise. Most experts agree that there are 4 to 5 common leadership styles. Directive leaders tell people what to do, how to do it and when it has to be done. Persuasive leaders use much the same style but they modify it a little by trying to use persuasion rather than being completely autocratic. Consultative leaders first get the opinions of others and then they, the leader, make the decision. Participative leaders not only obtain input from subordinates but ensure that decisions are made by consensus of the group. This means that any one member of the group has veto power over the decision. Lastly, delegative leaders turn over the entire task to a subordinate to perform including all decisions related to the task. Which one of these styles is best? That depends entirely on the task to be done, the skill, experience and maturity of the people doing it and the situation or circumstances surrounding the task. For example, no matter how skilled or mature people employees might be there can be crisis situations when a leader must make immediate autocratic decisions. Yet at other times with the same group when there are no time constraints, when full acceptance by all group members is essential and when a high degree of creativity or innovation is required then the leader may want to use a participative style.

45. Successful leaders are both people oriented and task oriented. There must be a proper balance between these two major considerations. A supervisor might be a "nice guy" but not focus sufficiently on getting the job done and there be highly ineffective as a leader. On the other hand, the highly skilled technical supervisor who places such heavy emphasis on getting the product or service completed that she is insensitive to the human concerns and needs of her subordinates will also be ineffective in the long run.

46. There are two terms that you should understand here which are highly relevant to this issue. They are authority and responsibility. Any appointed supervisor or leader has a certain amount of authority to make decisions, issue instructions and to otherwise accomplish their job. They are also held responsible for accomplishing their job, which includes the work product of their subordinates, in a certain manner and for producing certain results. You can think of authority as being power and responsibility as being obligation. Supervisors and leaders can delegate certain of their power or authority. This includes sharing with employees the power to make decisions. But, supervisors and leaders can never give away or even share their responsibility. They will always be held accountable for the final results that are expected of them, even if the cause for failure to achieve the results can be traced to errors or bad decisions on the part of their subordinates.

47. Most certainly that is a very important responsibility, one that would likely result in the termination of the supervisor if consistently not attained. However, supervisors as leaders have a very major responsibility to their subordinates, to people in other work units within the organization and in many cases to people outside of the organization like customers or vendors. Supervisors have the responsibility to treat their subordinates in a fair, uniform and consistent manner. They have the responsibility to serve as a critical link between the employees and higher management, especially regarding communication and feedback. Supervisors must deal with their peers in other work units in a constructive, collaborative way and they must ensure that the product of their work unit fully meets the customer's expectations. They must also deal with any vendors in a partnering way that represents the best interests of the employer and at the same time is fair and reasonable to the vendor.

48. Work assignments should be made on primarily on the basis of skill, ability and experience. Sometimes, as in the case of a labor agreement, work assignments must be made also on the basis of seniority - but never on the basis of friendships or on the basis of who will complain less about the assignment. Supervisors can be confronted with difficult situations like having an employee balk at accepting a less desirable work assignment In such cases supervisors should not take advantage of any past social or personal relationships in order to get the job done without a hassle. Pleading with an employee, calling upon past relationships or friendships in order to persuade an employee to follow a work order or using social relationships for that purpose are all totally unacceptable behavior and will tend only to quickly diminish the stature and effectiveness of the leader in the eyes of all of his or her subordinates.

49. If it were not possible for you personally to become a good leader, or a better one if you are already a good leader, they you would be wasting your time taking this training course. Yes, certain people seem to be natural leaders. But leadership is also an acquired skill that can be learned, developed and refined. While it may be true that some people simply may not have either the desire or capability of being a leader, most people can develop leadership skill if they make the effort.

50. Weak supervisors, poor leaders, often try to ingratiate themselves with employees by blaming higher management for unpopular decisions. For example, suppose an employee makes a request for an extra day off and the supervisor knows that the request cannot be granted due to a heavy work load. But, rather than be straightforward about it the supervisor says something like this: "Well, if it was up to me I'd have not problem letting you take the day off. But, I checked with my boss had he won't let me do it." There are many variations of this scenario and in all of them the supervisor has both diminished his or her own stature and leadership effectiveness and at the same time has made the company look bad.

T6 - Team Building

51. There is a significant difference between a group and a team. Groups are inevitable and teams are not. People form groups for many reasons, including simply their human need for affiliation. Most groups are characterized by a shared interest on the part of their members. Group members may share interests but not necessarily values or goals and objectives. Groups can be formal or informal. An example of a formal group would be a book club at a local library or a home and garden society. In both cases members share a common interest but not necessary common goals or values. An informal group might be 4-5 employees who regularly have lunch together in the company cafeteria or a half dozen people out of 20 in a customer service department who "pal around" together both at work and off the job.

    Teams share some of the same characteristics as groups including common interests. But in addition, in an effective team the members will also share the same values and goals and they will work together collaboratively toward accomplishing mutually agreed objectives. Because they are more structured than groups, teams are seldom informal. They are usually formed with a specific purpose in mind and generally function according to a mutually agreed set of procedures or ground rules. This is especially true in the work place where work teams have been specially appointed to accomplish very specific work related goals like improving product or service quality, developing a new design or improving work methods. Work teams can be heterogeneous consisting only of employees in a specific work unit or they can be heterogeneous having a cross-functional mix of employees from different departments, organizational levels or skill areas.

52. Teamwork is the process of cooperation and collaboration that takes place among individuals who are working together to accomplish a specific goal whether or not they have been appointed to membership on a team. Many organizations encourage teamwork among employees even though the organization has not established formal teams like productivity task teams or autonomous work teams. Further, do not mistake teamwork with team effectiveness. For example, consider an NFL football team. They might have all of the requisites of a formal team and at the same time demonstrate a high degree of teamwork. Yet in any particular game they simply cannot seem to coordinate their efforts properly or their communication is poor or there is some other problem that prevents them from being effective in that game no matter how hard they try or how committed they are to win. This illustrates that there is more to developing an effective team than just structure or desire.

53. Interpersonal relationship functions are those associated with establishing and maintaining harmonious, trustful relationships among team members. This includes team members encouraging and motivating each other, being friendly, amiably resolving disagreement, and ensuring that all members feel comfortable to participate fully in team discussions. Task performance functions focus on getting the job done. They include using a rationale problem solving or decision making process, keeping team discussions centered on the task at hand, adhering to schedules and producing quality results.

54. Conflict means disagreement. But, there is nothing inherently destructive about disagreement. In fact, disagreement is often highly constructive because it can create an atmosphere where people try to understand each other better and seek out better solutions to a problem. In that sense disagreement or conflict can be desirable. Conflict can also be destructive. However, when conflict does arise rather than suppress it a problem solving approach should be used, this involves open, candid communication, active listening on the part of all parties and an understanding of conflict resolution methodology.

55. Teams can be appointed quite easily. A manager might appoint a task team consisting of employees who have technical skills appropriate to the task at hand and who share the same interests, job values and results objectives. But that does not ensure that the team will function effectively. For example, suppose that this is the first time that any of the team members have worked together as a team. Perhaps they have all been individual contributors in the past and none have any team experience. In order for them to function effectively as a team there must be team building. The cornerstone of team building is increasing the team's awareness about how they function as a team -- their team process. Team process centers on the interpersonal relationship functions and task performance functions that are discussed elsewhere in this course.

56. In the sense of rewards and recognition teams work much like the process of empowerment. In empowerment rewards are shared among those who earned them at all organizational levels. This means that if a particular empowered work team accomplished a certain objective then the rewards for results attained would certainly be shared among those members of the team who made the results possible. It is entirely possible that the nature of what was accomplished was primarily the accomplishment of only one individual. In that case the individual would be recognized for the special contribution made. That is how the process of reward and recognition works for all team, as well.

57. This would be contrary to the principle that a team building is based on the strategy of making teams aware of how well they are functioning as a team. An effective team welcomes criticism and studies it objectively to seek out ways to improve itself. This is true whether criticism comes from within the team or from outside the team or whether it is levied toward only one member or the entire team.

58. Constructive competition can be useful. On a short term basis there is nothing wrong with contests or other forms of constructive competition that energizes people to generate ideas for improvement or to reach or beat certain performance goals. Besides, many such programs are a lot of fun and help to break up the monotony that exists in some structured work environments. But, employees must be encouraged to work collaboratively as a team and not just as a group of competent individual contributors if there is to be an atmosphere of true teamwork among them. Further, on a long term basis it has been shown that teamwork produces better, longer lasting results than competition -- no matter how friendly and fun.

59. This brings up the issue of team leadership in general. Leading teams requires special skills that some supervisors may not currently possess. You have learned elsewhere in this training course that today's supervisor, especially those who are supervisors in empowered work units, lead by coaching, facilitating, supporting and helping rather than by exercising traditional managerial control. This principle applies to team leaders in most other situations, as well. But, in addition, when a supervisor is meeting with a team of employees to solve a problem or make a decision still another skill is required -- the skill of leading a meeting or facilitative leadership. This is the ability of a meeting leader to clearly define the purpose and objective of a meeting with the team, establish meeting ground rules and procedural guidelines, guide the team as it uses both rational and creative problem solving techniques, ensure that all members are participating as fully as possible and remain focused on task accomplishment and results.

60. In almost any team at least one member can arrive at the "best" decision more quickly than the team and in some cases that person's decision is actually better or more effective than the team decision. Team decision making can definitely be slower than individual decision making. At the same time, when a team makes a decision, especially through the process of consensus, then the decision becomes the commitment of all team members. This is not at all necessarily the case when a decision is made by an individual contributor no matter how competent he or she may be. Further, studies show that the average team decision is usually better than the decision of the average individual on the team. And, when a team is functioning most effectively the team decision achieves the level of synergism. This means that the team decision is better than the decision of the best member on the team, a situation that occurs about 25% of the time that team decisions are made.

Part III   Post-Test

T   F

☐   ☐   1. The primary communication responsibility of supervisors is to pass important job related information downward to employees.

☐   ☐   2. The most effective form of communication is a carefully worded memo or letter.

☐   ☐   3. The listening effectiveness of the average person is only about 25%.

☐   ☐   4. Active listening is a term that describes a three step process for improving listening effectiveness.

☐   ☐   5. The "grapevine" is a useful and effective channel of communication in almost any organization.

☐   ☐   6. In order to improve work unit communication, supervisors should make a point of talking with employees about matters of legitimate interest to them such as company policy, work methods, sports, political, or religious matters.

☐   ☐   7. Much of the message content exchanged between people ion a face-to-face conversation is nonverbal in nature.

☐   ☐   8. Higher management should be the primary source of authoritative job-related information for employees in most organizations.

☐   ☐   9. One sign of an effective communication process is the absence or near absence of complaints or grievances.

☐   ☐   10. The single most important human interaction skill for a supervisor is the skill of effective listening.

T-1 Nr. Correct: _____

T	F	
☐	☐	11. In many cases what an employee complains about is not really what is bothering them.
☐	☐	12. Formal complaint or problem solving procedures should be avoided because they tend to limit a supervisor's ability to resolve issues that bother employees.
☐	☐	13. In most cases supervisors lack the authority to resolve an employee's problem or complaint.
☐	☐	14. Counseling employees about problems or complaints requires well developed listening skills.
☐	☐	15. Because "off-the-job" personal problems can affect an employee's performance at work, supervisors should always be willing to discuss these non-job related problems with them.
☐	☐	16. Coaching and counseling are the same thing.
☐	☐	17. In most cases supervisors should avoid being critical of an employee's job performance because employees generally resent being told that they are doing something wrong.
☐	☐	18. Coaching includes confronting an employee about job performance problems.
☐	☐	19. For the convenience of both the employee and the supervisor work related problems or complaints should be discussed promptly after they occur and at the employee's work station.
☐	☐	20. It is more difficult to change an employee's attitude or work behavior than it is to increase their job knowledge and skills.

T-2 Nr. Correct: _____

T	F	
☐	☐	21. Motivation is based on a person's needs or goals.
☐	☐	22. Once an important need has been fulfilled it no longer serves as a strong motivator.
☐	☐	23. Recognition is most effective when it is administered as soon as possible after a task is performed well.
☐	☐	24. Whether or not a supervisor is able to use motivation effectively or not depends largely on the nature of the job.
☐	☐	25. Employees who perform routine, repetitive, and monotonous tasks are usually less productive than those whose jobs are more fulfilling.
☐	☐	26. Administering discipline to an employee usually tends to lower work group motivation.
☐	☐	27. Studies show that pay is actually a potential dissatisfier -- not a true motivator.
☐	☐	28. Higher management is usually in a better position than the immediate supervisor to motivate employees.
☐	☐	29. In order for a reward to motivate an employee not only must it be important but the employee must also believe that it is attainable.
☐	☐	30. Motivation is the act of getting people to want to perform a task willingly and effectively.

T-3 Nr. Correct: _____

T	F	
☐	☐	31. Empowerment is based on the concept of shared responsibility.
☐	☐	32. Empowerment as a work practice can be used in most organizations anytime, under almost any circumstance.
☐	☐	33. In order for empowerment to exist all members of a work team must take part in making all of the decisions affecting the team.
☐	☐	34. Empowerment is more effective when the nature of the work to be done is highly structured rather than creative and open-ended.
☐	☐	35. One of the weaknesses of the empowerment concept is that the role of a leader becomes so unclear that management control can be lost.
☐	☐	36. Before an empowerment program can be successfully implemented there must be a high degree of trust and mutual respect between management and employees.
☐	☐	37. In order to optimize performance, supervisors of empowered work units should encourage friendly competition among their employees.
☐	☐	38. Empowered employees should be involved with setting their own performance goals but not with developing strategies for accomplishing departmental goals.
☐	☐	39. Empowerment does not work effectively when applied to culturally diverse groups of employees.
☐	☐	40. There are no formally appointed leaders in an empowered work force.

T-4 Nr. Correct: _____

T	F	
☐	☐	41. Leadership can be defined as the act of getting things done through others.
☐	☐	42. A leader cannot lead unless followers accept and follow his or her leadership.
☐	☐	43. Most successful leaders rely on the power of their appointed position to get things done.
☐	☐	44. The most effective leaders select a leadership style that suits them and use it consistently in any situation they encounter.
☐	☐	45. The most important focus of leadership is on people and on maintaining positive human relationships.
☐	☐	46. Employee involvement in decision making frees the leader from responsibility for the results of the decision.
☐	☐	47. A supervisor has only one major responsibility -- to get the job done according to standards set by his or her employer.
☐	☐	48. When confronted with difficult situations like having an employee balk at accepting a less desirable work assignment, supervisors should take advantage of any past social or personal relationships in order to get the job done without a hassle.
☐	☐	49. Good leaders are born -- not made.
☐	☐	50. In order to maintain their personal credibility supervisors should candidly tell employees about any organization policy or higher management decisions with which they (the supervisor) disagree.

T-5 Nr. Correct: _____

T	F	
☐	☐	51. In a work place a team is any informal group of employees who share a common interest.
☐	☐	52. Teamwork cannot exist unless employees are formed into formal teams.
☐	☐	53. There are two essential sets of functions that any effective team must perform, interpersonal relationship functions and task performance functions.
☐	☐	54. Conflict among members of a team is usually destructive and should be avoided if possible or suppressed if it does arise.
☐	☐	55. The primary strategy of team building is to increase the awareness of team members about their own process as a team.
☐	☐	56. A major problem with being part of a team is that individual accomplishments are no longer recognized.
☐	☐	57. Team loyalty requires that team members pull together to defend members against criticism by using techniques such as explaining, justifying and rationalizing.
☐	☐	58. Encouraging constructive competition between individuals in the same work unit will almost always help to foster a team spirit.
☐	☐	59. Team leaders should focus on building employee commitment rather than on building performance controls.
☐	☐	60. Team problem solving is usually a slower process than problem solving by competent individual contributors who may be working either as a member of the team or independent of the team.

T-6 Nr. Correct: _____

Post-Test Score			
Skill Area	Baseline Score	Post-Test Score	Gain/Loss
T-1			
T-2			
T-3			
T-4			
T-5			
T-6			
TOTAL			

Supervisory Skills Test

by
Louis E. Tagliaferri, Ph.D.

Administration Guide
MD-118ELG

SYNOPSIS

TITLE: SUPERVISORY SKILLS TEST

PURPOSE: To evaluate the cognitive skills of managers, supervisors and/or candidates for those positions.

DESCRIPTION: The Supervisory Skills Test (SST) is a 48 item objective test. This test measures the respondent's understanding of management and supervisory principles, practices and behaviors. A total of twelve crucial management and supervisory skill dimensions are evaluated.

VALIDITY: The content validity of the SST is based on extensive study and research that focused on identifying those skills, practices and behaviors that are required of essentially all managers and supervisors in order for them to be effective. The construct and design of the instrument ensures proper universe of content, simplicity of item wording, and minimization of such biases as acquiescence and social desirability.

ADMINISTRATION: Facilitator administered and scored.

APPLICATION: Training needs analysis.
                        Management and supervisory training.
                        Career counseling and development.

SUITABLE FOR: First level supervision through middle management.

SCORING: Manual scoring instructions will be found in this guide. Question set collation with correct answers are provided.

WHAT IT IS

The Supervisory Skills Test is designed to help HRD and Training Professionals assess the understanding of key employees about essential management and supervisory principles and practices. The test consists of 48 true/false items that measure the 12 skill dimensions listed below:

Planning & Organizing	Employee Discipline	Teamwork
Communication	Motivation	Leadership
Complaint Handling	Training	Time Management
Coaching & Counseling	Human Behavior	Problem Solving

The Supervisory Skills Test has many useful applications. It can be used as a pre and post evaluative tool in supervisory training programs; to help trainers measure training program effectiveness; to help develop training needs analysis data from which training programs can be constructed; or, the SST can be made part of an organization's career counseling program as it helps to identify developmental opportunities for employees who have current or prospective supervisory level responsibilities.

WHAT IT IS BASED ON

The SST is based on extensive literature research including a review of the theories of well known management scientists such as Herzberg, Maslow, Vroom, McGregor, Bennis, Skinner, Blake and Mouton and many others. Below are several of the many authoritative references that were used in the development of this questionnaire. Answers are based on the weight of opinion, research findings and conclusions presented by the authors/editors of this and other reference material.

1. Hersey, Paul and Blanchard, Kenneth H., Management of Organizational Behavior: Utilizing Human Resources, Englewood Cliffs, NJ, Prentice-Hall Inc., 1977.

2. Kinlaw, Dennis C., Coaching for Commitment: Managerial Strategies for Obtaining Superior Performance, San Diego, University Associates, 1989.

3. Prokopenko, Joseph and White, James (Eds), Modular Programme for Supervisory Development, Vols. 1-5, Geneva, Switzerland, International Labour Office, 1981.

4. Tosi, Henry L., and Hamner, W. Clay (Eds), Organizational Behavior and Management: A Contingency Approach, Chicago, St. Clair Press, 1976.

5. Tracy, Wm. R. (Ed), Human Resources Management & Development Handbook, New York, AMACOM, 1985.

6. Wexley, Kenneth N. and Yukl, Gary A., Organizational Behavior and Personnel Psychology, Homewood, IL, Richard D. Irwin, Inc., 1984.

HOW TO ADMINISTER AND SCORE IT

Distribute one copy of the Respondent Booklet to each person who is being tested. Explain the purpose of the questionnaire and the way results will be used. Read the instructions to the employees and answer any questions that they might have. Allow employees 30 minutes to complete the test.

The following are the questions sets for the SST together with the correct answer for each test item (T = True, F = False).

1.	Planning & Organizing	1-F,	13-T,	25-T,	37-F
2.	Communication	2-T,	14-F,	26-T,	38-F
3.	Complaint Handling	3-F,	15-F,	27-F,	39-T
4.	Coaching & Counseling	4-T,	16-T,	28-T,	40-T
5.	Employee Discipline	5-F,	17-T,	29-F,	41-T
6.	Motivation	6-T,	18-T,	30-F,	42-F
7.	Training	7-T,	19-T,	31-F,	43-T
8.	Human Behavior	8-T,	20-F,	32-T,	44-T
9.	Teamwork	9-F,	21-F,	33-T,	45-F
10.	Leadership	10-T,	22-F,	34-T,	46-T
11.	Time Management	11-F,	23-T,	35-F,	47-F
12.	Problem Solving	12-F,	24-T,	36-T,	48-T

More than two errors per question set may indicate a developmental need in that skill/knowledge dimension. Multiply the total number of correct answers by 2.083 to obtain the net score. Net test score norm is 77.4.

Test Score	Proficiency/Potential Level
90 -100	High
80-89	Above Average
70-79	Average
60-69	Below Average
Below 60	Low

Participant Booklet for

SUPERVISORY SKILLS TEST

by Louis E. Tagliaferri, Ph.D.

MD-118

| DATE: |
| ORGANIZATION: |
| WORK GROUP: |
| NAME: |

INSTRUCTIONS: The following are statements about management and supervisory functions, behavior and practices. Please read each statement carefully. Then indicate whether you believe that the statement is true or false by placing a mark in the appropriate column to the right.

STATEMENTS	True	False
01. The first step in the planning function is organizing the necessary resources.	☐	☐
02. The listening effectiveness of the average person is about 25%.	☐	☐
03. In order to reach a speedy solution, grievance discussions should be held at an employee's work station.	☐	☐
04. When coaching employees about job performance it is proper to confront them about performance problems.	☐	☐
05. Discipline is always punitive in nature and should only be used as a last resort.	☐	☐
06. Motivation is based on a person's needs or goals.	☐	☐
07. Training is the transfer of knowledge from one person to another.	☐	☐
08. Work is as natural as rest or play for the average employee.	☐	☐
09. In order for a team to be effective there must be an absence of conflict.	☐	☐
10. Leadership is getting things done through others.	☐	☐
11. Time management problems can usually be solved by doing things efficiently.	☐	☐
12. The first step in the problem solving process is to get the facts.	☐	☐
13. In order for an objective to be valid it must be measurable.	☐	☐
14. The "grapevine" is a useful communication channel in almost any organization.	☐	☐
15. In almost all cases a complaint accurately reflects the true nature of a grievance.	☐	☐
16. Coaching is a form of training.	☐	☐
17. Refusal or failure to obey the instructions of a supervisor is considered to be insubordination.	☐	☐
18. Recognition is most effective when it is administered as soon as possible after a job is performed well.	☐	☐
19. Most new, inexperienced employees are unaware of the extent of their incompetence regarding the job.	☐	☐

		True	False
20.	It is traditional for higher management to appoint the informal leader of a work group.	❑	❑
21.	Compromise and problem solving are both equally effective strategies for resolving conflict.	❑	❑
22.	The most effective leadership style is the participative management style.	❑	❑
23.	There is no way to save time; we can only use it.	❑	❑
24.	Logic, mathematics and convergent thinking are examples of the scientific problem solving method.	❑	❑
25.	Both forecasting and developing strategies are part of the planning process.	❑	❑
26.	Research has shown that the most important human relations skill a supervisor can have is listening.	❑	❑
27.	Most first level supervisors lack the authority to deal with the complaints of their employees.	❑	❑
28.	A primary characteristic of coaching is that it focuses on performance or on performance related subjects.	❑	❑
29.	It is unwise to discipline employees for work performance as long as their personal conduct is good.	❑	❑
30.	Higher management is usually in a better position to motivate employees than are first level supervisors.	❑	❑
31.	Any technically qualified senior employee can effectively conduct on-the-job training for new employees.	❑	❑
32.	The behavior of employees is affected as much by emotion as it is by logic and reason.	❑	❑
33.	Synergism occurs when the team product is greater than the product of all of the individuals on the team.	❑	❑
34.	A leader cannot lead unless the followers accept the leader's leadership.	❑	❑
35.	Effective delegation allows a supervisor to retain close control over the details of the delegated task.	❑	❑
36.	Problem solving focuses on the past while decision making focuses on the future.	❑	❑

		True	False
37.	Planning is a function for higher management while scheduling is a function for supervisors.	☐	☐
38.	The major source of job related information for employees should be higher management.	☐	☐
39.	The best way to deal with an emotional complaint is to listen and let the employee "blow off steam".	☐	☐
40.	Coaching differs from counseling in that coaching also involves confronting employees about performance.	☐	☐
41.	Progressive discipline involves increasing disciplinary measures for repeated violations of work rules.	☐	☐
42.	Recognition, achievement, pay and status are examples of true motivators.	☐	☐
43.	It is easier to increase knowledge than skill and it is easier to change attitude than behavior.	☐	☐
44.	Human relations practices have a greater effect on morale than on productivity.	☐	☐
45.	Constructive, friendly competition is an excellent way to develop teamwork.	☐	☐
46.	The "best" leadership style depends on the nature of the job, on the people doing it and on the situation.	☐	☐
47.	A good way to save time is to look for short cuts in performing management functions.	☐	☐
48.	Basically, the same methods are used to make decisions and to solve problems.	☐	☐

Team Communication
Effectiveness Assessment

by
Louis E. Tagliaferri, Ph.D.

Facilitators Guide
TB-402ELG

SYNOPSIS

PURPOSE:

The purpose of the **Team Communication Effectiveness Assessment** (TCEA) is to help members of work teams critique and improve the quality and effectiveness of their task related communication skills.

DESCRIPTION:

TCEA is a 25 item learning and feedback instrument with a Likert response scale. The instrument helps work team members evaluate their perceptions about the quality of communication within their team in 5 sets of measurement dimensions: relevancy, utility, trust, openness and inclusion.

VALIDITY:

Content and construct face validity have been established through literature research and field correlation studies regarding group dynamics and the process of communication in work teams. Scale construction has minimized ambiguity, social desirability, acquiescence and other biases.

FACILITATION:

Self-administered and self-scored. Requires about 15 to 20 minutes.

APPLICATION:

Excellent for team building, communication training, work team development, management and supervisory training.

SUITABLE FOR:

Any organizational level.

WHAT IT IS

TCEA is a learning and feedback instrument that is designed to help work team members improve the quality and effectiveness of team communication. It provides work team members with a basis by which they can assess conditions that affect work team communication including related group process behaviors. Researchers have long known that in order for communication within a team to be effective it must meet certain criteria. Communication must be open, honest and candid. It must be relevant to the team's task, such as problem solving or making a team decision. Team members must feel comfortable "exposing" their thoughts, feelings and perceptions and must avoid dysfunctional behaviors such as withholding information for the purpose of gaining power or for other manipulative purposes.

Task related information must be timely, accurate and sufficient to get the job done. It is also crucial to have full and complete participation by all work team members and a team climate that encourages their ideas and suggestions.

The 5 measurement dimensions covered by the TCEA are:

Relevancy -- the extent to which information is relevant and meaningful to the team's task.

Utility -- the extent to which the work team acquires and processes information that is timely, accurate and sufficient to get the job done.

Trust -- the extent to which the work team shares mutual trust and respect and maintains constructive interpersonal relationships.

Openness -- the extent to which communication among work team members is open, honest and candid.

Inclusion -- the extent to which all members of the work team demonstrate behaviors which encourage full team participation and facilitate effective problem solving and decision making discussions.

HOW TO ADMINISTER IT

One copy of the TCEA is required for each member of the work team. A facilitator (either a member of the team or an outside specialist) should introduce the exercise, explain its purpose and ensure that all team members understand how to complete the instrument. The facilitator should also ensure that all team members understand the feedback process which will be used with the TCEA and what outcomes are expected from the exercise.

The TCEA can be scored separately by the facilitator or by the team together as part of the communication skills improvement intervention.

HOW TO SCORE IT

In order to score the TCEA first calculate the percent positive response for each TCEA item among your team population. **Both** "Strongly Agree" **and** "Somewhat Agree" are considered positive responses. The percent positive response for each item is determined by dividing the number of "Strongly Agree" and "Somewhat Agree" responses by the number of the respondents on your team and then multiplying the quotient by 100. Next, record the percent positive response for the 25 items in the appropriate space below:

Relevancy		Utility		Trust		Openness		Inclusion	
Item	Score	Item	Score	Item	Score	Item	Score	Item	Score
01	____	02	____	03	____	04	____	21	____
05	____	06	____	07	____	08	____	22	____
09	____	10	____	11	____	12	____	23	____
13	____	14	____	15	____	16	____	24	____
17	____	18	____	19	____	20	____	25	____
Set Score		**Set Score**		**Set Score**		**Set Score**		**Set Score**	
____		____		____		____		____	

The "Set Score" is calculated by averaging the percentages for all items in each set.

HOW TO INTERPRET IT

The following guidelines will help team members interpret the results of the TCEA and plan for ways by which they can improve their problem solving abilities.

Score	**Interpretation Guideline**
80-100	Team communication skills are well developed. The team currently seems to have the communication skills needed to perform its task effectively.
70-79	Team communication skills are reasonably well developed but opportunities for improvement exist. Currently, team communication efforts should be at least moderately successful.
60-69	Team communication skills may be only marginal. Improvement in more than one communication skill dimension is needed in order for the team's communication efforts to be consistently successful.
Below 60	Improvement in team communication skills may be urgently needed. The effectiveness of the team's current communication efforts is questionable.

Participant Booklet

Team Communication
Effectiveness Assessment

by Louis E. Tagliaferri, Ph.D.

TB-402EPB

DATE:	
ORGANIZATION:	
WORK GROUP:	
NAME:	

Instructions: The following are 25 statements about conditions that can occur when members of work teams meet to discuss work related matters. Please read each statement carefully. Think of the condition as it might apply to your own work team. Then indicate the extent that you agree or disagree with each statement by placing a mark in the appropriate column to the right. The response scale abbreviations correspond with the following: **SA=Strongly Agree**, **A=Agree**, **?=Uncertain**, **D=Disagree**, **SD=Strongly Disagree**.

		SA	A	?	D	SD
01.	Most of the information shared among members of our work team is relevant to the team's task.	[ ]	[ ]	[ ]	[ ]	[ ]
02.	We usually have sufficient information to deal with the team task effectively.	[ ]	[ ]	[ ]	[ ]	[ ]
03.	All of the members of our work team respect each other.	[ ]	[ ]	[ ]	[ ]	[ ]
04.	Communication among members of our work team is usually frank and honest.	[ ]	[ ]	[ ]	[ ]	[ ]
05.	The average member of our work team usually has something meaningful to contribute to the team's discussion.	[ ]	[ ]	[ ]	[ ]	[ ]
06.	We receive current and timely information about the task that our work team is assigned.	[ ]	[ ]	[ ]	[ ]	[ ]
07.	The members of our work team trust each other.	[ ]	[ ]	[ ]	[ ]	[ ]
08.	The members of our work team deal with each other in a fair and honest way.	[ ]	[ ]	[ ]	[ ]	[ ]
09.	When solving a problem or making a decision most of our work team's discussion focuses on the task at hand.	[ ]	[ ]	[ ]	[ ]	[ ]
10.	Most of the information we receive about our work team's task is accurate.	[ ]	[ ]	[ ]	[ ]	[ ]
11.	The members of our work team get along well with each other.	[ ]	[ ]	[ ]	[ ]	[ ]
12.	Members of our work team openly express their feelings, concerns and opinions.	[ ]	[ ]	[ ]	[ ]	[ ]
13.	Our work team usually deals with issues that can have an important affect on the team's task.	[ ]	[ ]	[ ]	[ ]	[ ]
14.	We usually have fully sufficient information to do the team's task properly.	[ ]	[ ]	[ ]	[ ]	[ ]
15.	The quality of interpersonal relationships among members of our work team is high.	[ ]	[ ]	[ ]	[ ]	[ ]

		SA	A	?	D	SD

16. There are few secrets among the members of our work team.
[ ] [ ] [ ] [ ] [ ]

17. The information that the members of our work team share with each other is seldom trivial or irrelevant to our main objective.
[ ] [ ] [ ] [ ] [ ]

18. It is unusual for us to have a problem with the accuracy or timeliness of the task related information we obtain.
[ ] [ ] [ ] [ ] [ ]

19. When conflict arises among members of our work team it is usually resolved through problem solving.
[ ] [ ] [ ] [ ] [ ]

20. The members of our work team feel free to speak up and express their views and opinions candidly.
[ ] [ ] [ ] [ ] [ ]

21. All the members of our work team fully participate in the discussions that we have about the team's task.
[ ] [ ] [ ] [ ] [ ]

22. Members of our work team make a point to solicit ideas and suggestions about the team's task from each other.
[ ] [ ] [ ] [ ] [ ]

23. We all listen carefully to what each member of the team has to say.
[ ] [ ] [ ] [ ] [ ]

24. We recognize members of our work team when they have an especially good idea.
[ ] [ ] [ ] [ ] [ ]

25. The members of our work team equally share responsibility for facilitating discussion about the team's task.
[ ] [ ] [ ] [ ] [ ]

Team Leader
Skills Assessment

by
Louis E. Tagliaferri, Ph.D.

Facilitators Guide
TB-408ELG

SYNOPSIS

TITLE: TEAM LEADER SKILLS ASSESSMENT (TLSA)

PURPOSE:

1.   To provide managers, supervisors and team leaders with feedback about the extent to which they may engage in behaviors characteristic of those used by superior team builders.

2.   To provide managers, supervisors and team leaders with self-assessment information that will help them improve their team building skills.

DESCRIPTION:

The TLSA is a self-assessment instrument that measures the extent to which the respondent may engage in eight sets of practices that research has shown are focus issues of superior team builders: Action, Performance, Improvement, Contact, Relationships, Development, Team Interaction and Personal Character. The instrument consists of sixteen forced choice pairs of practices. Respondents are required to select the specific practice that is most applicable to them.

VALIDITY:

This instrument is based on research that has been conducted throughout industry by several noted management authorities. In the design of the instrument every reasonable effort was made to ensure proper universe of content, simplicity of wording and the minimization of such biases as acquiescence and social desirability. Face validity was further established through the use of this instrument in a field test among a group of 39 first line supervisors, middle managers and project team leaders.

ADMINISTRATION: Self or facilitator administered. Requires 15 to 20 minutes.

APPLICATION: Team Leader Skill Development
Team Building
Management Development
Career Development
Performance Coaching

SUITABLE FOR: Any manager, supervisor or team leader and/or candidates for those positions.

CONCEPTUAL BACKGROUND

Early studies on the subject of team building leadership tended to concentrate on the personal characteristics and traits of team builders and on their personal leadership styles. Most of these studies were more concerned with what team leadership is rather than how it works; or, more specifically, with what it is that successful team builders do.

More current research has focused on identifying patterns of behavior that can distinguish the truly successful team builders from those who are less successful. This recent research has led to several important and interesting conclusions. One major finding is that the truly successful team builders place considerable emphasis on transforming employees from groups of individual contributors into highly effective work teams that produce synergistic results. They accomplish this not because of their traits or characteristics, or even because of their particular leadership style. Rather, they are successful team builders because they regularly engage in a set of behaviors that combines a focus on the achievement of performance excellence with a focus on the development of team interaction skills.

Several noted management researchers (Bennis [1989], Fiedler [1983], Harris [1989] and Yukl [1971] among others) have found clear patterns of behavior that identify superior, high performing managers and supervisors. In almost all cases, superior managers and supervisors were also superior team builders. One of the most persuasive findings is presented by Kinlaw (1989) as he describes eight sets of practices that, by extensive research and field testing in the aerospace industry, clearly distinguish superior team builders from others. The development of the TEAM LEADER SKILLS ASSESSMENT has been strongly influenced by this latter research.

The eight sets of practices measured by the TLSA together with the questionnaire item numbers are:

1. **ACTION (1-2):** The team builder gets things done, solves problems and overcomes organizational obstacles.

2. **PERFORMANCE (3-4):** The team builder strives for performance excellence for both self and work team. The team builder ensures that employees know what is expected of them and how well they are meeting those expectations.

3. **IMPROVEMENT (5-6):** The team builder continually works with employees as a team to creatively and innovatively identify ways by which improvement can be achieved.

4. **CONTACT (7-8):** The team builder maintains close contact and open communication with employees and with key people in other work units.

5. **RELATIONSHIPS (9-10):** The team builder ensures that harmonious work relationships are maintained with others and constructively resolves conflict.

6. **DEVELOPMENT (11-12):** The team builder places emphasis on developing new skills and competencies both for self and for members of the work team.

7. **TEAM INTERACTION (13-14):** The team builder is a team player who involves team members in important decision making activities.

8. **PERSONAL CHARACTER (15-16):** The team builder sets a personal model of conduct and behavior for employees to follow.

HOW TO ADMINISTER AND SCORE IT

The TEAM LEADER SKILLS ASSESSMENT is a self-scoring instrument that is extremely easy to interpret. Scoring instructions will be found on the back cover of the Respondent Booklet.

Participants will obtain optimum value from the instrument if it is used in connection with either a team building intervention or with a team leadership training program. It is also excellent as part of a supervisory training program where the focus is on developing skills for transforming work units into successful work teams.

After the questionnaire is completed and scored by the respondent, the facilitator should define the meaning of the eight sets of practices and briefly conduct a group discussion about the principles and concepts upon which the instrument is based. The following recommended reading section will be useful for facilitators who are not currently familiar with the relevant concepts and principles.

RECOMMENDED READING

1. Bennis, Warren, Why Leaders Can't Lead, San Francisco, Jossey-Boss Publishers, 1989.

2. Fiedler, Fred E. and Chemers, Martin M., Improving Leadership Effectiveness 2nd Ed., New York, John Wiley & Sons, Inc., 1983.

3. Harris, Philip R., High Performance Leadership: Strategies for Maximum Career Productivity, Glenview, IL, 1989.

4. Kinlaw, Dennis C., Coaching for Commitment, San Diego, University Associates Inc., 1989.

5. Yukl, G. A., Toward a Behavioral Theory of Leadership. Organizational Behavior and Human Performance, 1971, 6, 414-440.

Participant Booklet

For The

Team Leader
Skills Assessment

TB-408

By
Louis E. Tagliaferri, Ph.D.

TEAM LEADER SKILLS ASSESSMENT

INSTRUCTIONS

Below are 16 pairs of practices that are common to many leaders of teams and work groups. Read each pair of practices carefully. Then place a mark in the space to the left of the one practice in each pair that best describes your own practices. If both practices seem to apply to you, then select the one that is <u>most</u> applicable to you.

___ 1a. Takes prompt action to deal with problems and other critical situations.

___ 1b. Approaches problems and other critical situations cautiously and deliberately.

___

___ 2a. Uses personal contacts to overcome organizational obstacles and get things done.

___ 2b. Uses the formal systems and procedures of the organization to get things done.

___

___ 3a. Makes sure that employees know what performance standards are expected of them and how well they are meeting those standards.

___ 3b. Prefers that performance standards for employees be self-directed and self-measured.

___

___ 4a. Sets very high goals and standards for self and employees.

___ 4b. Concentrates on accomplishing important, attainable goals.

___

___ 5a. Encourages employees to suggest ways by which operations can be improved.

___ 5b. Uses feedback from employees to help maintain established performance standards.

___

___ 6a. Meets with employees to discuss creative and innovative ways by which costs can be reduced.

___ 6b Meets with employees to ensure that they clearly know and understand current work group goals and objectives.

___

___ 7a. Seeks out occasions to informally talk with all employees.

___ 7b. Maintains an "open door" policy for all employees.

___ 8a. Ensures that there is an open exchange of job related information within the work group and with other work groups.

___ 8b. Avoids communication problems within the work group and with other work groups by ensuring that formal communication channels are followed.

———————————

___ 9a. Uses effective and harmonious methods to resolve conflict.

___ 9b. Uses tact and discretion when expressing own ideas and feelings.

———————————

___ 10a. Prefers to maintain an informal relationship with employees and peers.

___ 10b. Maintains good relationships with others by respecting the chain of command.

———————————

___ 11a. Seeks out new challenges that require developing new skills.

___ 11b. Prefers to master current challenges and expand current expertise.

———————————

___ 12a. Ensures that employees are trained to develop new skills.

___ 12b. Ensures that employees understand their current responsibilities.

———————————

___ 13a. Achieves the greatest success as a member of a team.

___ 13b. Achieves the greatest success as the leader of a work group.

———————————

___ 14a. Involves employees in making decisions that affect the work group.

___ 14b. Delegates work group decision making to qualified employees.

———————————

___ 15a. Uses own technical competence as a model for employees.

___ 15b. Requires that employees perform their jobs in a competent manner.

———————————

___ 16a. Displays own work standards and value systems openly.

___ 16b. Requires honesty and integrity from all employees.

HOW TO SCORE IT

The TEAM LEADER SKILLS ASSESSMENT measures the extent to which you may engage in practices which are characteristic of superior team leaders, including managers and supervisors. Eight sets of practices are covered by the instrument. These practices are listed below together with the numbers of the questionnaire items which comprise each set.

ACTION (1-2)	RELATIONSHIPS (9-10)
PERFORMANCE (3-4)	DEVELOPMENT (11-12)
IMPROVEMENT (5-6)	TEAM INTERACTION (13-14)
CONTACT (7-8)	PERSONAL CHARACTER (15-16)

In all cases choice "a" is the alternative which is most characteristic of superior team leaders. A maximum of 16 points is possible. Use the following scale to rate yourself:

15-16	Excellent
13-14	Very Good
11-12	Good (Norm = 12)
9-10	Fair
0-8	Needs improvement

The facilitator who administered this instrument will define the eight sets of practices for you and will suggest ways by which you can further improve your team building skills.

Team Member
Behavioral Analysis

by
Louis E. Tagliaferri, Ph.D.

Facilitators Guide
TB-404ELG

SYNOPSIS

Purpose: The purpose of the **Team Member Behavior Analysis** (TMBA) is to familiarize work team members with both constructive and dysfunctional team behaviors, and to provide them with feedback about how their personal behaviors are perceived by and affect other team members.

Description: The TMBA is a 40 item, multi-level learning and feedback instrument that measures respondents' perceptions about the team related behaviors of individual work team members. The 40 items are categorized into 10 sets of 4 items each. Five sets measure constructive behaviors and 5 measure dysfunctional behaviors.

Validity: Content and construct face validity have been established through literature research and field correlational studies regarding group process, work team interaction, group dynamics and group norms and by ensuring a scale design that minimized biases such as ambiguity, acquiescence, and social desirability.

Facilitation: Self-administered. Requires 20 to 25 minutes.

Application: Team building, work team development, management and supervisory training.

Suitability: All organizational levels.

Scoring: A reproducible scoring format will be found on the back cover of this guide.

WHAT IT IS

The TMBA is based on models of team participation which categorize team members by the behaviors they display when working on a team task. Research suggests that there are 5 types of constructive behaviors desirable for team members and 5 types of behaviors that are dysfunctional. These behaviors can be described as follows:

Initiator -- the person who gets the "ball rolling" and who helps the team define its mission, goals and objectives.

Facilitator -- a team member who acts as a catalyst for discussion and who ensures that ideas, suggestions, opinions and relevant information are openly and candidly shared.

Motivator -- an encourager who uses praise and recognition to stimulate the team to achieve its full potential.

Harmonizer -- the person who helps keep the team's interpersonal relations at a high quality level, even when the going gets rough.

Analyzer -- who critically evaluates the team's performance and who helps ensure that the team focuses on its assigned task.

The 5 dysfunctional behaviors are:

Child -- whose lack of interest and fooling around detracts from the positive efforts of other team members.

Aggressor -- a team member whose tough behavior can intimidate others.

Monopolizer -- one who dominates the team discussion, wrestles control from the legitimate leader and who talks endlessly without making a real contribution.

Resister -- the classic "can't get there from here" person whose negativism blocks and undermines the more positive work of other team members.

Hermit -- who either deliberately or from shyness withholds participating in the team discussion and who makes little or no contribution to the team effort.

Obviously, it is essential for members of work teams to focus on the constructive behaviors and to minimize or eliminate those which are dysfunctional. Feedback to team members based on the TMBA can be very useful in making work teams aware of the existence of these behaviors and to provide them with data upon which they can base strategies for improvement. (Note: It is possible for an individual team member to display more than one of the above behaviors.)

HOW TO ADMINISTER IT

The TMBA has been designed in a multi-level format to enhance its value. This format allows more than one observer to assess the behaviors of individual work team members. Best results will be obtained if work team members assess themselves and are concurrently assessed by either a team facilitator and/or by other members of the work team.

The facilitator should first explain the purpose of the TMBA to respondents and then read the instructions to them. Be sure that all team members clearly understand who they are to assess and how the TMBA is to be completed.

Allow up to 30 minutes for the TMBA to be completed and then collect and score the questionnaires. (See scoring format on the back cover of the TMBA questionnaire.) Feedback of his/her scores can be given confidentially to each team member who was assessed or, if codes are used instead of names, they can be shared with the entire team. A brief discussion by a facilitator about the alternative behaviors measured by the TMBA, together with coaching and discussion about ways by which individual team members can improve their team behavior, will add further value to the exercise.

RECOMMENDED READING

Austen, W.G. and Worschel, S. (Eds), The Social Psychology of Intergroup Relations, Monterey, CA, Brooks-Cale, 1979.

Buchholz, Steve and Roth, Thomas, Creating the High Performance Team, New York, John Wiley & Sons, Inc., 1987.

Cribbin, James J., Leadership, New York, AMACOM, 1981, pp. 156-172.

Fisher, Ronald J., Social Psychology: An Applied Approach, New York, St. Martin's Press, 1982, Chapters 5-9.

Harper, Bob and Harper, Ann, Succeeding As A Self-Directed Work Team, Croton-on-the-Hudson, NY, MW Corporation, 1989.

Kinlaw, Dennis C., Developing Superior Work Teams, San Diego, University Associates, 1991.

Kinlaw, Dennis C., Team-Managed Facilitation, Critical Skills for Developing Self-Sufficient Teams, San Diego, Pfeiffer & Company, 1993.

Shaw, M.E., Group Dynamics: The psychology of small group behavior, (3rd Ed), New York, McGraw-Hill, 1981.

HOW TO SCORE IT

The TMBA can easily be scored by following these steps:

1. Make a photocopy of this page for each set of individual team member scores you will require.

2. Point values are:

   * Very Characteristic = 5
   * Generally Characteristic = 4
   * Moderately Characteristic= 3
   * Generally Uncharacteristic = 2
   * Not Characteristic At All = 1

3. Total the self-ratings made by the individual team member for each set of 4 items; i.e. for items 01-04, etc. Record these ratings in the appropriate space in each scoring column. Repeat this process for ratings made by the individual team member's superior.

4. Average the totals for each set of 4 items from the questionnaires of the subordinates/peers (SUB/PEER) and record the averaged totals in each scoring column as you did in # 3 above.

5. Total each scoring column. Record the total in the appropriate space in each scoring column.

6. Team member behavior styles or types may have a significant affect on team performance when the total in a scoring column (like for **Initiator**) is 36 or greater. (When the employee is assessed by only two levels the threshold score is 24.)

7. Be sure to carefully study the ratings among the three rating levels to identify any significant perceptual differences that might exist. Significant perceptual differences could indicate lack of candor or poor communication among team members, interpersonal conflict or similar problems.

8. Individual team member scores can be transferred to the Scoring Format on the back cover of the Participant's Booklet in order to facilitate discussion about behavior patterns.

Team Member Name: _____

SCORING COLUMNS (Enter scores here)

Initiator (01-04)

Self: —

Superior: —

Sub/Peer: —

Total: —

Facilitator (05-08)

Self: —

Superior: —

Sub/Peer —

Total: —

Motivator (09-12)

Self: —

Superior: —

Sub/Peer: —

Total: —

Harmonizer (13-16)

Self: —

Superior: —

Sub/Peer: —

Total: —

Analyzer (17-20)

Self: —

Superior: —

Sub/Peer: —

Total: —

Child (21-24)

Self: —

Superior: —

Sub/Peer: —

Total: —

Aggressor (25-28)

Self: —

Superior: —

Sub/Peer: —

Total: —

Monopolizer (29-32)

Self: —

Superior: —

Sub/Peer: —

Total: —

Resister (33-36)

Self: —

Superior: —

Sub/Peer: —

Total: —

Hermit (37-40)

Self: —

Superior: —

Sub/Peer: —

Total: —

Participant Booklet for

Team Member Behavior Analysis

by Louis E. Tagliaferri, Ph.D.

TB-404EPB

DATE:	
ORGANIZATION:	
WORK GROUP:	
NAME:	

Instructions: The following are behaviors and practices that have been found to exist among members of work teams. Please decide the extent to which you believe that these behaviors are characteristic of the person whose name appears on the front cover of this questionnaire when he or she is engaged in discussions with other members of your work team. Then indicate your decision by circling the appropriate point value in the rating column to the right of each behavior or practice.

Rating Scale Values: 1 = Not characteristic at all; 3 = Moderately characteristic; 5 = Very characteristic, etc.

To what extent does the named person:

01.	Suggest new issues for the team to discuss?	1 2 3 4 5
02.	Help the team to decide on goals or objectives?	1 2 3 4 5
03.	Introduce a new method or procedure for completing a task?	1 2 3 4 5
04	Recommend a new approach for dealing with a problem?	1 2 3 4 5
05.	Help keep a meaningful discussion going?	1 2 3 4 5
06	Act as a catalyst for constructive team discussions?	1 2 3 4 5
07.	Ask for clarification of facts?	1 2 3 4 5
08.	Seek out the opinions of other team members?	1 2 3 4 5
09.	Praise or otherwise recognize the work of other team members?	1 2 3 4 5
10.	Stimulate others to greater team participation?	1 2 3 4 5
11.	Acknowledge the value of other team members' contributions?	1 2 3 4 5
12.	Encourage the team to achieve its full potential?	1 2 3 4 5
13.	Help reduce tension when the going gets tough?	1 2 3 4 5
14.	Smooth out any lack of harmony within the team?	1 2 3 4 5
15.	Mediate conflict within the team?	1 2 3 4 5
16.	Help keep team relationships positive?	1 2 3 4 5
17.	Assess the success of the team's efforts?	1 2 3 4 5
18.	Evaluate the quality of the team's interpersonal relationships?	1 2 3 4 5

To what extent does the named person:

19.   Suggest ways by which the team can improve its performance?   1 2 3 4 5

20.   Critique the way the team deals with problems?   1 2 3 4 5

21.   Display lack of interest in the team task?   1 2 3 4 5

22.   Give the impression that he/she is bored?   1 2 3 4 5

23.   Fool around and distract other members of the team?   1 2 3 4 5

24.   Tell jokes and "kid around" or play tricks on others?   1 2 3 4 5

25.   Display tough, aggressive behavior?   1 2 3 4 5

26.   Verbally attack other members of the team?   1 2 3 4 5

27.   Use ridicule and intimidation to get his/her way?   1 2 3 4 5

28.   Try to control the team discussion by using fear tactics?   1 2 3 4 5

29.   Interrupt others at every opportunity?   1 2 3 4 5

30.   Try to dominate by manipulating the team?   1 2 3 4 5

31.   Talk endlessly about meaningless things?   1 2 3 4 5

32.   "Wrestle" with the leader for control of the team?   1 2 3 4 5

33.   Oppose almost everything?   1 2 3 4 5

34.   Display a negative attitude toward the team's task?   1 2 3 4 5

35.   Have an "it can't be done" attitude?   1 2 3 4 5

36.   Undermine and block the team's progress?   1 2 3 4 5

37.   Remain silent throughout most team discussions?   1 2 3 4 5

38.   Contribute little to the team's effort?   1 2 3 4 5

39.   Listen a lot and remain passive during team meetings?   1 2 3 4 5

40.   Behave in a very quiet and shy manner?   1 2 3 4 5

SCORING FORMAT

Instructions: Sum the score for the items within each category for each work team member. Record the scores in the appropriate spaces below. For example, for Team Member #1 (TM#1) sum the rated point values of items 1-4 and record that sum in the **Initiator** row under the **TM#1** column. Then, for the same team member, sum the rated point values for items 5-8 and record that sum in the **Facilitator** row under the **TM#1** column, etc. The minimum score at which team member behavior patterns begin to be established is 24 within a behavior type set for two level ratings and 36 for three level ratings.

BEHAVIOR TYPE	TM#1	TM#2	TM#3	TM#4	TM#5	TM#6	TM#7	TM#8	TM#9	TM#10
Initiator Items 1-4										
Facilitator Items 5-8										
Motivator Items 9-12										
Harmonizer Items 13-16										
Analyzer Items 17-20										
Child Items 21-24										
Aggressor Items 25-28										
Monopolizer Items 29-32										
Resistor Items 33-36										
Non-Participator Items 37-40										

Copyright Louis E. Tagliaferri, Ph.D. 1987-2003

152

Team Problem Solving Skills Assessment

by
Louis E. Tagliaferri, Ph.D.

Facilitators Guide
TB-405ELG

SYNOPSIS

PURPOSE:
The purpose of the **Team Problem Solving Skills Inventory** (TPSSI) is to provide members of work teams with feedback about the problem solving processes which they are using and to help improve their problem solving skills.

DESCRIPTION:
The TPSSI is an easy-to-use learning and feedback instrument that consists of 30 items with a Likert type response scale. Items are categorized into 5 sets of 6 items each which measure perceptions about how effectively work team members engage in these key problem solving skill dimensions: systematic methods, statistical processes, creativity and innovation, information processing, work team interaction.

VALIDITY:
Content and construct face validity have been established through literature research and from data obtained through field correlational studies of employee work teams including cost improvement teams, productivity task teams, and continuous improvement quality teams. Scale design has minimized biases such as ambiguity, social desirability, and acquiescence.

FACILITATION:
Can be facilitator administered or self-administered by team members. Requires 15-20 minutes.

APPLICATION:
Developing problem solving and decision making skills, team building and work team development.

SUITABLE FOR:
All organizational levels.

SCORING:
Manually scored. Refer to scoring section in this guide.

What it is

In business, industry or government the typical work team is a processing unit. The unit receives inputs from other work teams, processes these inputs and transforms them into outputs in the form of products or services. The products or services of a work team are for the benefit of its customers, internal or external. In order for the work team's products or services to have value (to be of benefit to the customer) they must conform with standards established by or for its customers. In other words, they must meet the customer's expectations. This principle is true whether the work team is an accounting or design department, a manufacturing or assembly unit, or special task team such as a continuous improvement team.

In the course of performing the tasks necessary to meet its customers' requirements, a work team is continually confronted with the need to make decisions and to solve problems. This is because no work process is perfect and, consequently, it is inevitable that variations in product and service quality (variation from customer expectations) exist. Variation leads to problems which must be solved and to decisions which must be made. Work teams must also deal with and solve "problems" in the form of continuous improvement opportunities and challenges.

A learning and feedback instrument, the **Team Problem Solving Skills Inventory** (TPSSI) measures a work team's assessment of how effectively it engages in 5 sets of behaviors, practices and conditions which are known to affect team problem solving. Dimensions measured are:

*   **Systematic Methods** (Items 1-6) -- the extent to which a work team follows a rational, systematic approach to problem solving; i.e. the "scientific method."

*   **Statistical Processes** (Items 7-12) -- the extent to which a work team understands statistical methods and uses statistical tools to collect and analyze problem solving data.

*   **Creativity & Innovation** (Items 13-18) -- the extent to which a creative climate exists within a work team and to which a work team understands and applies creative problem solving methods.

*   **Work Team Interaction** (Items 19-24) -- the extent to which a work team's interaction behavior supports and facilitates empowered problem solving.

*   **Information Processing** (Items 25-30) -- the extent to which team problem solving is facilitated by the flow, sufficiency, openness, timeliness and accuracy of task related information.

TPSSI can be used for self-analysis by a work team or for facilitator guided team building interventions. Additional value will be gained if TPSSI data are also obtained from other organizational units which are affected by the work team's problem solving efforts.

How to Score it

In order to score the TPSSI first calculate the percent positive response for each TPSSI item among your team population. **Both** "Strongly Agree" **and** "Somewhat Agree" are considered positive responses. The percent positive response for each item is determined by dividing the number of "Strongly Agree" and "Somewhat Agree" responses by the number of the respondents on your team. Next, record the percent positive response for the 30 items in the appropriate space below:

Systematic Methods		Statistical Processes		Creativity & Innovation		Work Team Interaction		Information Processing	
Item	Score	Item	Score	Item	Score	Item	Score	Item	Score
01	____	07	____	13	____	19	____	25	____
02	____	08	____	14	____	20	____	26	____
03	____	09	____	15	____	21	____	27	____
04	____	10	____	16	____	22	____	28	____
05	____	11	____	17	____	23	____	29	____
06	____	12	____	18	____	24	____	30	____
Set Score		**Set Score**		**Set Score**		**Set Score**		**Set Score**	
____		____		____		____		____	

The "Set Score" is calculated by averaging the percentages for the six items in each set.

How to Interpret it

The following guidelines will help team members interpret the results of the TPSSI and plan for ways by which they can improve their problem solving abilities.

Score	Interpretation Guideline
80-100	Team problem solving skills are well developed. The team currently seems to have the problem solving skills needed to perform its task effectively.
70-79	Team problem solving skills are reasonably well developed but opportunities for improvement exist. Currently, team problem solving efforts should be at least moderately successful.
60-69	Team problem solving skills may be only marginal. Improvement in more than one problem solving skill dimension is needed in order for the team's problem solving efforts to be consistently successful.
Below 60	Improvement in team problem solving skills may be urgently needed. The effectiveness of the team's current problem solving efforts is questionable.

Participant Booklet

Team Problem Solving
Skills Inventory

by Louis E. Tagliaferri, Ph.D.

TB-405EPB

DATE:	
ORGANIZATION:	
WORK GROUP:	
NAME:	

Instructions: Below are 30 behaviors, practices and conditions which can affect work team problem solving efforts. Please read each item carefully. Decide the extent to which each item is characteristic of problem solving activities within your work team. Indicate your decision by placing a mark in the appropriate column to the right of each item. For purposes of the rating scale, **SA**=Strongly Agree, **SW**=Somewhat Agree, **?**=Unsure, **SW**=Somewhat Disagree, **SD**=Strongly Disagree.

Problem Solving Behaviors	**SA**	**SW**	**?**	**SW**	**SD**
01. When confronted with a problem the team first ensures that the problem or decision issue is clearly defined.	[ ]	[ ]	[ ]	[ ]	[ ]
02. Team members thoroughly gather the facts about the task to which they are assigned.	[ ]	[ ]	[ ]	[ ]	[ ]
03. Before looking for a solution the team ensures that it has accurately identified the problem root cause.	[ ]	[ ]	[ ]	[ ]	[ ]
04. When trying to solve a problem the team first imagines all possible alternative solutions and their ramifications.	[ ]	[ ]	[ ]	[ ]	[ ]
05. The team is careful to evaluate the advantages and disadvantages of alternative solutions to the problem.	[ ]	[ ]	[ ]	[ ]	[ ]
06. Decisions regarding the best solution for a problem are usually based on the consensus of all team members.	[ ]	[ ]	[ ]	[ ]	[ ]
07. All members of the team understand the quantitative and qualitative standards required in order to meet customer requirements.	[ ]	[ ]	[ ]	[ ]	[ ]
08. All members of the team have been trained in the use of statistical problem solving methods.	[ ]	[ ]	[ ]	[ ]	[ ]
09. The team regularly uses data analysis tools such as Pareto Analysis, Histograms, Control Charts and Cause-Effect Analysis.	[ ]	[ ]	[ ]	[ ]	[ ]
10. The team uses statistical methods to identify causes of variation from standard for the team's task.	[ ]	[ ]	[ ]	[ ]	[ ]
11. Statistical Quality Control is used by the team in order to ensure that it's products/services meet customer expectations.	[ ]	[ ]	[ ]	[ ]	[ ]
12. The team regularly uses analytical tools to study its work processes and identify opportunities for improvement.	[ ]	[ ]	[ ]	[ ]	[ ]
13. There is a great deal of restlessness among the team to explore new new problems or challenges.	[ ]	[ ]	[ ]	[ ]	[ ]
14. Team members display a strong sense of independent judgement.	[ ]	[ ]	[ ]	[ ]	[ ]

Problem Solving Behaviors   SA SW ? SW SD

15.   Team members encourage each other to develop creative or innovative   [ ] [ ] [ ] [ ] [ ]
      solutions to problems.

16.   All members of the team have been trained in creative problem solving   [ ] [ ] [ ] [ ] [ ]
      methods and techniques.

17.   Within the team "wild" or "far out" ideas are welcome, even if there   [ ] [ ] [ ] [ ] [ ]
      is no immediate application for them.

18.   Team members are free to choose whatever problem solving methods   [ ] [ ] [ ] [ ] [ ]
      or systems they believe are best.

19.   Team members listen to each other in a way that shows empathy or   [ ] [ ] [ ] [ ] [ ]
      understanding.

20.   There is a great deal of mutual support and encouragement among   [ ] [ ] [ ] [ ] [ ]
      members of the team.

21.   Responsibility for producing quality results is shared equally among   [ ] [ ] [ ] [ ] [ ]
      all members of the team.

22.   All members of the team participate fully in team activities like decision [ ] [ ] [ ] [ ] [ ]
      making and problem solving.

23.   The team frequently critiques how well it is performing its task   [ ] [ ] [ ] [ ] [ ]
      including how well its members interact with each other.

24.   The responsibility for leading or facilitating discussion and problem   [ ] [ ] [ ] [ ] [ ]
      solving is shared equally among all members of the team.

25.   Decision making information is shared openly among all team members.   [ ] [ ] [ ] [ ] [ ]

26.   Communication among team members is candid and honest.   [ ] [ ] [ ] [ ] [ ]

27.   The team ensures that its members are provided with all of the   [ ] [ ] [ ] [ ] [ ]
      information they need to do their job properly.

28.   Accurate task related information is made available to team members   [ ] [ ] [ ] [ ] [ ]
      on a timely basis.

29.   Team members share, evaluate and process task related information in   [ ] [ ] [ ] [ ] [ ]
      an objective manner.

30.   Team members are skilled at using data and information to understand   [ ] [ ] [ ] [ ] [ ]
      and solve problems and to make decisions.

Self-Directed
Team Assessment

by
Louis E. Tagliaferri, Ph.D.

Facilitators Guide
TB-406ELG

PURPOSE:

The **Self Directed Team Assessment (SDTA)** is designed to help members of work teams learn and apply behaviors and practices which will facilitate total quality team performance.

DESCRIPTION:

A learning and feedback instrument, the SDTA consists of 30 items with a 5 point rating scale. The instrument measures perceptions about how effectively a work team engages in 6 sets of team performance behaviors, practices and conditions: active listening, inclusion, processing information, sharing responsibility, solving problems and focusing on continuous improvement.

VALIDITY:

Content and construct validity have been established through literature research and from data obtained through field correlational studies of continuous improvement task teams. Scale design has minimized biases such as ambiguity, social desirability, and acquiescence.

FACILITATION:

Can be facilitator administered or self-administered by team members. Requires 15-20 minutes.

APPLICATION:

Continuous improvement teams, total quality action teams, self-directed work teams, empowerment training, general team building and management and supervisory training.

SUITABLE FOR:

All organizational levels.

SCORING:

Manually scored. Refer to scoring section at the end of each SDTA questionnaire.

WHAT IT IS

The classic Hawthorne studies first demonstrated the potential value of group participation and support as means by which work performance and, consequently, productivity can be improved. Since the early Hawthorne experiment there have been many studies and experiments in participative management, worker involvement activities and, most recently, in work team oriented continuous improvement and total quality management programs. It has long been observed that participation in work related issues can increase employee satisfaction and productivity. However, it has been only recently that definitive work has been done to determine exactly which conditions in the work environment facilitate total quality team performance.

The SDTA is based upon the findings of these studies. It consists of 30 items, statements, each of which represent an important behavior, practice or condition related to successful work team performance. The behaviors, practices and conditions assessed by the SDTA are based on the Malcolm Baldrige Quality Award criteria and upon the findings of noted work team development researchers.

The SDTA measures work team member perceptions about the following team performance dimensions:

- Active Listening
- Processing Information
- Inclusion
- Sharing Responsibility
- Solving Problems
- Focusing on Continuous Improvement

Active Listening is a skill in which team members listen to each other in a non-evaluative way, acknowledge another's views and respond to the message sender in a way that shows understanding or empathy and that obtains additional information.

The skill of **Processing Information** is related to **Active Listening** but also involves ensuring that the team gathers, shares, and processes sufficient, timely and accurate information that is relevant to the work team task.

Inclusion is the process of encouraging and obtaining the active participation of all work team members in the team's decision making and problem solving efforts. It requires ensuring that all of the team's human resources are utilized to the fullest possible level.

Sharing Responsibility is a key empowerment concept which means that each member of the work team has responsibility to ensure that the team engages in constructive task and interpersonal relations behaviors. It also involves the process of inclusion, ensuring that all team members fully participate in the team activity, and it involves rewards sharing.

Solving Problems is a major reason why work teams exist. In order to do this, they must know, understand and apply systematic problem solving methods including both scientific and creative methods.

Finally, in order to achieve total quality team performance, work teams must **Focus on Continuous Improvement** by continuing to develop their problem solving skills, improving their team interaction processes and by evaluating the extent to which they meet or exceed quality performance goals and objectives.

HOW TO ADMINISTER IT

The SDTA can be either facilitator or self-administered. One copy of the SDTA is required for each member of the work team. After all team members have completed the questionnaire one member should be appointed as recorder of the scores, using the scoring format on the back cover of each questionnaire. Scored data should then be fedback to all team members and should be used as the basis for discussion regarding opportunities to improve the work team's performance to total quality team performance levels.

RECOMMENDED READING

Beardsly, Jefferson F., Quality Circles, Human Resources Development Handbook, AMACOM, 1985, pp.326-340.

Bederan, Arthur G., Organization: Theory and Analysis, Hinsdale, IL. The Dryden Press, 1980.

Brown, Mark Graham, Baldridge Award Winning Quality: How to Interpret the Malcolm Baldrige Award Criteria, White Plains, NY, Quality Resources, Milwaukee, WI, Quality Press, 1991

Fisher, Ronald J., Social Psychology: An Applied Approach, New York, St. Martin's Press, 1982. pp 235-377.

Katz, Daniel and Kahn, Robert L., The Social Psychology of Organizations (2nd ed), New York, John Wiley & Sons, 1978.

Kinlaw, Dennis C., Continuous Improvement and Measurement for Total Quality: A Team-Based Approach, San Diego, Pfeiffer & Company/Business One Irwin, 1992.

Kinlaw, Dennis C., Developing Superior Work Teams: Building Quality and the Competitive Edge, San Diego, University Associates, 1991.

Margulies, Newton and Black, Stewart, Perspectives on the Implementation of Participative Approaches, Human Resource Management, Fall 1987. No. 3, pp 385-405.

Participant Booklet

Self-Directed
Team Assessment

by Louis E. Tagliaferri, Ph.D.

TB-406EPB

DATE:
ORGANIZATION:
WORK GROUP:
NAME:

Instructions: Below are six sets of team behaviors that can affect the performance of work teams. Read each item carefully. In the column to the left, enter the value that indicates the extent that you believe the behavior exists within your work team **Now**. Next, enter the value that indicates the improvement **Goal** for each behavior that you believe your work team should establish for the near term future. Use the following scale for your response: 1 = Very Little; 2 = Little; 3 = Some; 4 = Considerable; and 5 = Very Considerable for both the **Now** and **Goal** ratings.

Active Listening -- When a member of our team speaks, other members ....

Now   *Goal*

____ ____   01.   are attentive and show interest in what he or she is saying.

____ ____   02.   ask questions for the purpose of clarifying what was said.

____ ____   03.   probe to obtain additional information.

____ ____   04.   respond in a way that shows empathy or understanding.

____ ____   05.   listen to what is said before evaluating and judging.

____ ____   **Totals**

Processing Information -- All of the members of our work team ....

Now   *Goal*

____ ____   06.   share task related information openly and honestly.

____ ____   07.   provide each other with candid, constructive feedback.

____ ____   08.   evaluate task related information objectively, without bias.

____ ____   09.   ensure that task related information is timely and accurate.

____ ____   10.   focus on factual information -- not speculation.

____ ____   **Totals**

Inclusion -- Each member of our work team ....

Now   *Goal*

____ ____   11.   encourages other members to offer their ideas and suggestions.

____ ____   12.   respects the dignity and self-worth of other members.

____ ____   13.   expresses appreciation to other members for their efforts.

____ ____   14.   gives other members a chance to demonstrate their expertise.

____ ____   15.   helps other members participate fully in all team activities.

____ ____   **Totals**

Sharing Responsibility -- Each member of our work team ....

Now　　*Goal*

____　____　16.　shares the workload in a fair and equitable manner.

____　____　17.　takes personal responsibility for achieving quality results.

____　____　18.　shares the role of leading and facilitating team discussions.

____　____　19.　helps maintain harmonious relationships among all team members.

____　____　20.　shares recognition the team receives for its accomplishments.

____　____　**Totals**

Solving Problems -- When working on a task our team ....

Now　　*Goal*

____　____　21.　focuses on the real problem or decision issue.

____　____　22.　follows a systematic problem solving method.

____　____　23.　demonstrates effective team interaction skills.

____　____　24.　understands and uses creative techniques.

____　____　25.　has the technical skills required to deal with the task.

____　____　**Totals**

Focusing on Continuous Improvement -- Our work team ....

Now　　*Goal*

____　____　26.　regularly critiques how well it is performing the team task.

____　____　27.　openly looks for ways by which it can improve its effectiveness.

____　____　28.　consistently achieves high quality results.

____　____　29.　places emphasis on continually developing members' skills.

____　____　30.　is determined to find an even better way to do things.

____　____　**Totals**

HOW TO SCORE IT

1. Rating scale values are as follows:

1 = Very Little	3 = Some	5 = Very Considerable
2 = Little	4 = Considerable	

2. Total the **Now** and **Goal** scores for each team skill set. Then average the set scores for all members of your team.

3. Record the average scores for each skill set in the appropriate columns in the scoring template.

4. Determine the variance or difference between the **Now Avg** and the **Goal Avg**. Record the differences in the **Variance** column.

5. Team skill set **Now** average totals less than 20 and/or variances greater than 5 may indicate that the work team is performing below its desired performance level with respect to the relevant behaviors, practices or conditions.

6. Use the team skill set average and variance data to identify the major performance barriers that your work team is experiencing. Then, work as a team to develop strategies to overcome these performance barriers.

SCORING TEMPLATE

Team Skill Set	Now Avg	Goal Avg	Variance
Active Listening	_____	_____	_____
Processing Information	_____	_____	_____
Inclusion	_____	_____	_____
Sharing Responsibility	_____	_____	_____
Solving Problems	_____	_____	_____
Focusing on Continuous Improvement	_____	_____	_____

Time Management Inventory

by
Louis E. Tagliaferri, Ph.D.

Administration Guide
MD-112ELG

TITLE:	TIME MANAGEMENT INVENTORY

PURPOSE:
1) To develop consciousness and awareness about the importance of proper time utilization.
2) To teach key time management principles.

DESCRIPTION: The Time Management Inventory (TMI) is a unique learning instrument that will help managers, supervisors and employees at any level improve their time and self-management practices. The instrument places emphasis on planning, prioritization, scheduling, work organization and delegation. Learning is attained by a critique of responses to twenty five "test" items together with a study of corresponding time management tips. A time management planning guide helps respondents develop strategies that will overcome major time management barriers that may be affecting their work.

VALIDITY: It is designed to facilitate learning rather than measure knowledge, skill or behavior per se. Validation is not applicable.

APPLICATION:
1) Time Management Training.
2) Performance Coaching and Counseling.

SUITABLE FOR: All levels.

Administration Guidelines

The TMI is a versatile instrument that is very easy to administer. Many organizations use the TMI either to kick off or to close a time management training module, seminar or workshop. Others use it as a supplement to other time management training material or as a short learning exercise to emphasize or reinforce important time management principles.

In order to administer the TMI, you should distribute one copy of the instrument to each participant. Read the instructions and answer any questions that employees might have. Allow about 25 - 30 minutes for the employees to answer all the questions. Then conduct a critique and discussion of all 25 TMI items. Be sure to read and discuss the TIME MANAGEMENT TIPS found in this Administration Guide. The number of each tip corresponds with the questionnaire item number.

Next, refer to the TIME MANAGEMENT PLANNING GUIDE. Randomly select employees from the group and ask them to read and explain what they have written in this section. Alternatively, have employees complete the latter section in teams. Then conduct a group discussion about each team's responses. In this case, the barriers and strategies should focus on broader organizational issues rather than on an individual's personal situation.

Time Management Tips

1. Prioritize your daily work. This is a major principle of time management that you should regularly follow. Use the "ABC" system. "A" is for the "must do" tasks. "B" is for the "should do's", and "C" is for dispensable tasks.

2. Do it right the first time. It is true that you can learn from mistakes. However, much time can be wasted by carelessness or by taking dangerous shortcuts.

3. Prepare for and group outgoing telephone calls. Consider allocating a certain period of time at the end of each morning and afternoon to make outgoing calls. Then, prepare your message and be brief. This makes effective use of the telephone.

4. Set aside time for creative thinking. You can do this while commuting, in between meetings, or during a short period of time scheduled for this purpose each day. This will improve your creative capacity and will help you to be innovative in your planning and scheduling activities.

5. Fail to listen carefully. This is a major barrier to effective time utilization. The average person's listening effectiveness is only 25%. If you improve your listening skills, you will improve time usage by avoiding mistakes, misunderstandings, etc.

6. Remain brief on incoming calls. Be polite, tactful and helpful, but, be brief. Avoid wasteful and unnecessary conversation.

7. Prepare and use meeting agenda. Poorly run meetings waste everybody's time. A well planned and followed agenda can shorten your meeting and improve its quality at the same time.

8. Develop plans for long-range projects. Planning is the first step in the management cycle or process. It is critical if you are to effectively manage your time and that of your subordinates.

9. Allow time for the unexpected. No matter how well you plan, the unexpected (problems, delays, etc.) will arise. If you plan too tightly, the unexpected will throw your entire schedule off.

10. Do things that really don't matter. Busy work or doing low priority ("C") tasks might make you look efficient, but, in reality, it makes you ineffective.

11. Tackle too many tasks at one time. This is usually the result of failure to prioritize and poor planning. It obviously is wasteful.

12. Personally open your own mail. The issue is not status but rather time effectiveness. A secretary can save you substantial time by opening your mail and screening out the "junk" mail.

13. Work with unclear instructions. This will cause you to lose time rechecking with your boss or, possibly, will result in mistakes and rework.

14. Fail to complete one task before starting another. This relates to prioritizing and planning, again.

15. Fail to prepare for meetings. Having an agenda is not enough. If you fail to properly prepare for the meeting, you probably will be wasting both your time and that of your fellow meeting participants.

16. Systemize your work. After you prioritize your daily tasks, you will benefit from thinking about the best, most effective way you can go about performing them.

17. Procrastinate. What you put off today really will hurt you tomorrow. Problems seldom go away. Decisions must be made. Do it when it needs to be done.

18. Do everything yourself. Failure to delegate is a major failing of many managers and, it wastes time because the manager performs tasks which interfere with the tasks of greater importance he or she should be doing.

19. Keep a time log. Try it for a week or two. Record all of the activities you engage in during a period of time. Review the log for time wasters.

20. Tackle the uncontrollable. Tackling the difficult is a challenge. Tackling the impossible is a waste of time.

21. Deal with symptoms - not problem causes. This is a major time waster. The problem will never be solved until you deal with its real cause. Anything less is a waste of time.

22. Give poor instruction. Same problem as getting poor instruction but in reverse.

23. Try to involve everyone. Participative management is a good practice - when appropriate. When not, it wastes your time and that of others. Involve only those who really need to be involved.

24. Never say no, and you will be inundated with unnecessary work. Don't try to be a "nice guy" and please everyone. Prioritize, plan and schedule.

25. Constantly work late or take work home. It is possible that you are overworked. More likely, though, this is a symptom of poor planning.

Participant Booklet for

TIME
MANAGEMENT
INVENTORY

by Louis E. Tagliaferri, Ph.D.

MD-112

| DATE: |
| ORGANIZATION: |
| WORK GROUP: |
| NAME: |

TIME MANAGEMENT PRACTICES

INSTRUCTIONS: This is a learning instrument rather than a test. Read each of the time management practices listed below. Then indicate whether you follow that practice frequently, sometimes or seldom by placing a check mark in the appropriate column to the right of each practice. After you have completed all 25 items please complete the **Time Management Planning Guide**. The person who is administering this instrument will then give you further instructions.

Time Management Practices	Frequently	Sometimes	Seldom
01. Prioritize your daily work.	❐	❐	❐
02. Do it right the first time.	❐	❐	❐
03. Prepare for and group outgoing telephone calls and e-mail.	❐	❐	❐
04. Set aside time for creative thinking.	❐	❐	❐
05. Fail to listen carefully.	❐	❐	❐
06. Remain brief on incoming telephone calls.	❐	❐	❐
07. Prepare and use meeting agenda.	❐	❐	❐
08. Develop plans for long - range projects.	❐	❐	❐
09. Allow time for the unexpected.	❐	❐	❐
10. Do things that really don't matter.	❐	❐	❐
11. Tackle too many tasks at one time.	❐	❐	❐
12. Personally open your own mail.	❐	❐	❐
13. Work with unclear instructions.	❐	❐	❐
14. Fail to complete one task before starting another.	❐	❐	❐
15. Fail to prepare for meetings.	❐	❐	❐
16. Systemize your work.	❐	❐	❐
17. Procrastinate.	❐	❐	❐
18. Do everything yourself.	❐	❐	❐

	Frequently	Sometimes	Seldom
19. Keep a time log.	❏	❏	❏
20. Tackle the uncontrollables.	❏	❏	❏
21. Deal with symptoms - not causes of problems.	❏	❏	❏
22. Give poor instructions.	❏	❏	❏
23. Try to involve everyone.	❏	❏	❏
24. Never say no.	❏	❏	❏
25. Constantly work late or take work home.	❏	❏	❏

TIME MANAGEMENT PLANNING GUIDE

1. List the three time management barriers that currently have the most serious affect on your work.

_____

_____

_____

_____

_____

_____

_____

2. Ideally, what would you like to see different about each of the above three barriers? Be as specific as possible.

_____

_____

_____

_____

_____

_____

_____

3. In the space below write the specific strategies that you can use to overcome each of the three time management barriers that you identified above. Be sure to include a target completion date.

a. _____

_____

_____

_____

b. _____

_____

_____

_____

c. _____

_____

_____

_____

4. What resources assistance will you require in order to implement the above strategies?

_____

_____

_____

_____

_____

_____

_____

_____

Training Needs
Assessment Test

by
Louis E. Tagliaferri, Ph.D.

Administration Guide
MD-129ELG

Training Needs Assessment Test
Administration Guide

by Louis E. Tagliaferri, Ph.D.

MD-129LG

Training Needs Assessment Test

Purpose: To evaluate the training needs of employees in key job related management and leadership attributes, behaviors and skills.

Description: Version 3.0 of the Training Needs Assessment Test consists of 75 objective test items that measure the respondent's understanding of management and supervisory principles, practices and behaviors. A total of fifteen key management and supervisory skill dimensions are evaluated. The instrument uses a Likert type response scale.

Validity: The content validity of the TNAT is based on field study and literature research that focused on identifying those skills, practices and behaviors which are required of most people who have leadership responsibility. The construct and design of the instrument ensures proper universe of content, simplicity of item wording, and minimization of such biases as acquiescence and social desirability. Normative data was obtained from field testing among mixed male/female populations of managers and supervisors from both public and private organizations.

Administration: Preferably facilitator administered. Can be self-administered if desired. Requires about 30 minutes.

Application:
* Training needs analysis.
* Management and supervisory training.
* Career counseling and development.

Suitable For: Leaders or candidates for leadership positions at any organizational level. This test is for developmental purposes only and is not intended as a pre-employment or screening type test.

Scoring: Completely self-scoring.

What It Evaluates

The TNAT evaluates a person's understanding about management and supervisory principles, practices and behaviors in the following fifteen crucial skill dimensions:

Coaching & Counseling: The supervisor's responsibility for coaching and counseling, coaching as a developmental process focusing on job performance, coaching to confront subordinates about performance issues, counseling employees about problems, complaints or grievances.

Communication: The supervisor's responsibility to communicate effectively, the nature and process of communication, communication channels, listening skills.

Employee Discipline: The purpose and objective of discipline, progressive discipline, the supervisor's responsibility to administer discipline, principles of administering discipline.

Empowerment: Empowerment concept and principles, shared responsibility, involvement and teamwork, facilitative leadership.

Human Relations: The concept of human relations, human relations supervisory techniques, the effects of human relations practices on morale and productivity, fairness, consistency and uniformity.

Leadership: The basic concept of leadership, leadership as a power of influence, leadership styles and characteristics, situational leadership.

Motivation: The supervisor's responsibility to motivate employees, the nature of motivation, how motivation works, understanding the affects of motivation on job performance.

Performance Management: Setting and communicating job standards, evaluative and developmental performance counseling, performance appraisal, understanding job satisfaction in relation to job performance.

Planning & Organizing: Anticipating future events, setting precise, measurable and realistic objectives, developing plans and strategies to accomplish objectives, identifying and gathering the resources necessary to put plans into action.

Problem Solving/Decision Making: Problem solving versus decision making, problem solving and decision making steps, creative problem solving.

Quality & Continuous Improvement: Fully meeting customers' needs and expectations, prevention versus detection, responsibility for quality work, employee participation in continuous improvement.

Team Building: Team interaction and group process, team effectiveness and conflict, synergistic team work, team work and competition.

Time Management: The basic concept of time management, eliminating time wasters, time management principles, delegation.

Training: Principles of learning, effective vs. ineffective training methods, measurement of training results.

Work Assignments: Work assignments and performance standards, work assignment fairness, the basis for making work assignments, ensuring that employees understand work assignments.

How to Administer It

The TNAT is purchased in sets of ten Respondent Booklets. Be sure that you have enough booklets for each employee who is to be tested. You should also have at least one office copy for your records. Begin the test administration process by first explaining the purpose and objectives of the test exercise to all participants. Explain how test results will be utilized and what process will be followed to provide employees with feedback information about their test results. Next, distribute one copy of the Respondent Booklet to each employee. Request that they write their name and organization in the appropriate spaces on the front cover of the test booklet. Additional codification on the front cover is optional when the test is administered to larger populations within the organization.

It is recommended that the test be administered to respondents under proctored conditions in controlled areas. Read the instructions for the test to the group. Ask for and answer any procedural questions, then instruct participants to begin the test. There is no time limit but most individuals will complete the test in about 30 minutes. After respondents have completed the test collect the booklets before they leave the controlled area.

How to Score It

A reproducible Personal Test Profile, including scoring grids and interpretation information, is included in the Appendix of this administration guide. Use the reproduced copy to record the respondent's TNAT scores and as a feedback instrument that can be given to the person. Following are instructions for scoring the test and for completing the Personal Test Profile for each test respondent.

1. The respondent's Personal Test Profile includes one scoring grid for each measurement dimension of the TNAT. Each measurement dimension consists of five (5) individual test items. In the measurement dimension of Coaching & Counseling, for example, the individual test items are numbers 1-5. In Communication they are 6-10 and so on. There is also a composite scoring grid in which summary scores for measurement dimensions or sets of items can be plotted.

2. Circle the response scale letter(s) or the symbol "?" in each scoring grid that corresponds with the letter(s) or symbol circled by the respondent in the test booklet for all test items. Response scales are to the right of each item number in the scoring grids. Note that although in the test booklet all scales follow the same sequence (**A SA SD D ?**), the scale sequence for the items in the scoring grids will vary. Be careful that you exactly match the circled letter(s) or symbol in the test booklet with those in the scoring grids.

3,   Add the number of circled response letters or symbols in each vertical **Response** column. Columns are identified as (a), (b), (c), (d), and (e). Multiple the total number of circled responses in each column by the factor shown, i.e. by 3, 2, 1 or 0. Then total the scores of each vertical column and write the sum in the column marked "**Set Score.**"

4.   Plot the set scores for each measurement dimension on the **Composite Score Grid**. Connect the plotted points to form a line graph for easier interpretation.

5.   Reproduce one set of the TNAT Personal Test Profile Interpretation Guide for each test respondent. The guide should be given to the respondent along with his/her test results.

6.   For test results interpretation purposes, individual measurement dimension or set scores below **10** suggest training needs. Even if a set score is **10** or above, an individual item score below **2** may suggest a training need in that particular skill attribute.

7.   When the TNAT is administered to groups of employees measurement dimensions or set scores may be averaged in order to identify "in common" training needs.

How to Feed Back Test Results

Most organizations administer the TNAT so that training needs profiles for individuals can be prepared. In order to optimize the value of the TNAT it is recommended that individual respondents be provided feedback about their test results. Best results will be obtained if TNAT results are personally reviewed with individual test respondents either by a qualified HRD professional or by the test respondent's supervisor or manager. The focus of the feedback session should be developmental -- not evaluative. These who are providing the feedback should use the respondent's Personal Test Profile as a "jumping off point" to discuss a variety of job performance and career development issues with the respondent. The respondent's TNAT scores should be compared with any available observations, perceptions, and objective information about the former's actual on-the-job performance. The end result should be a consensus decision about a developmental oriented action plan for the person.

How It Was Developed

The following information concerns the development, validity, purpose and application of the Training Needs Assessment Test (TNAT):

1.   The purpose of the TNAT is to evaluate "a person's understanding about management and supervisory principles, practices and behaviors" in a specified set of skill dimensions. Results of the TNAT are to be used, as the instrument's title suggests, for training needs analysis purpose. The TNAT is not a predictive instrument nor should it be used to draw conclusions about a person's job performance. It is to be used strictly for developmental purposes.

2.   The TNAT was developed by Louis E. Tagliaferri, Ph.D. Dr. Tagliaferri has over 30 years' experience as an MD and OD practitioner. He has extensive experience in assessment instrument design and development, in conducting in-depth developmental assessments of managers and supervisors and in designing and conducting management and supervisory training programs.

3.   The content validity of the TNAT is based on field study and literature research that focused on identifying those skills, practices and behaviors that are required of most successful managers, supervisors and other leaders. The construct and design of the instrument ensures proper universe of content, simplicity of item wording, and minimization of such biases as acquiescence and social desirability. In their work *Principles of Research in Social Psychology*, Crano and Brewer state the following about content validity:

> "Content validity is determined by the degree to which the items constituting the scale represent all possible positions on the domain under consideration."

There are no statistical procedures to establish content validity. Rather, as Wexley and Yukl point out in their text *Organizational Behavior and Personnel Psychology* "The determination of this type of validity is made on the basis of the judgement of 'experts' ..."

4.   The correct answers for the TNAT are based on thorough study of the discipline and through literature research including the following works, among many others:

*   Baker, Frank, Organizational Systems: General Systems Approach to Complex Organizations, Richard D. Irwin, Inc., Homewood, IL, 1973.

*   Blake, Robert R. and Mouton, Jane Srygley, The Managerial Grid, Gulf Publishing Co., Houston, 1964.

*   Buchholz, Steve and Roth, Thomas, Creating a High Performance Team, John Wiley & Sons, Inc., 1987.

*   Cribbin, James J., Leadership: Strategies for Organizational Effectiveness, AMACOM, New York, 1981.

*   Fiedler, Fred E. and Cheers, Martin M., Improving Leadership Effectiveness, John Wiley & Sons, Inc., New York, 1984.

*   Hampton, David R., Summer, Charles E., and Webber, Ross A. (E's), Organizational Behavior and the Practice of Management, Scott Foresman & Co., Glenview, IL, 1968.

* Harris, Philip R., High Performance Leadership, Scott Foresman & Co., Glenview, IL, 1989.

* Heresy, Paul and Blanchard, Kenneth H., Management of Organization Behavior: Utilizing Human Resources (3rd ed), Prentice-Hall, Inc., Englewood Cliffs, NJ, 1977.

* Kinlaw, Dennis C., Coaching for Commitment, University Associates, San Diego, 1989.

* Kinlaw, Dennis C., The Practice of Empowerment, Gower Publishing Limited, London, 1995.

* Prokopenko, Joseph and White, James (E's), Modular Programme for Supervisory Development, Vols 1-5, International Labour Organization, Geneva, 1981.

* Swanson, Richard A., Analysis for Improving Performance, Berrett-Koehler Publishers, San Francisco, 1994.

* Tagliaferri, Louis E., Successful Supervision, John Wiley & Sons, Inc., New York, 1979.

* Tagliaferri, Louis E., Creative Cost Improvement for Managers, John Wiley & Sons, Inc., New York, 1981.

* Zenger, John H., Musselwhite, Ed, Hurson, Kathleen and Perrin, Craig, Leading Teams, Business One Irwin, Homewood, IL, 1994.

5. A composite set of normative data based on a randomly selected population of managers (male and female, business, industry and government) have been compiled and is included in this guide. Respondents' scores can be compared against arithmetic means derived from these data.

6. As pointed out earlier, the TNAT assesses the respondent's understanding about various management and supervisory principles. It does not assess the extent to which a respondent applies this knowledge. It is entirely possible for incongruity to exist between a person's knowledge about a certain skill area and his or her actual work practice or behavior. For example a person may know and understand the concepts of interpersonal communication but may not have developed certain communication application skills, like the skill of effective listening. Conversely, a person may intuitively demonstrate positive human relations skills without understanding the underlying theories.

Because of this the most accurate assessment of training needs will be obtained when the TNAT is used together with instruments such as the Talico Inc. *Management Training Needs Analysis, Management Practices Inventory* or *Leadership Skills Test*, which are measurements of perceived work behaviors and practices.

7.   Whenever instruments are used to help assess developmental needs optimum accuracy will be obtained by using a parallel process of instrument assessment accompanied by personal interviews with the person who is being assessed. In all cases interpretation of assessment data should be done by a person who has the required management and organization development expertise.

TRAINING NEEDS ASSESSMENT TEST
Answer Scales

Following are fifteen sets of items that comprise the TNAT measurement dimensions. The most correct response for each item is in Column (a).

(a) (b) (c) (d) (e)

Coaching and Counseling

1. Coaching involves confronting employees about job performance problems.
    A SA SD D ?

2. It is more appropriate for an employee to be counseled about a job related problem by an organization's personnel or human resource department than by the employee's supervisor.
    D SD SA A ?

3. The best way for a supervisor to handle an emotional complaint by an employee is to first listen carefully and allow the employee to "blow off steam."
    A SA SD D ?

4. A sign of a smoothly running work unit is the absence of complaints.
    D SD SA A ?

5. Coaching, counseling and mentoring are interchangeable terms that describe the same managerial function.
    D SD SA A ?

Communication

6. The communication process is not complete until the message receiver acknowledges receipt and understanding of the message.
    A SA SD D ?

7. Department meetings, policy manuals, the "grapevine" and bulletin board notices are all examples of formal communication channels.
    D SD SA A ?

8. The most effective form of communication is a graphic illustration that is supplemented by a written explanation of the illustration.
    D SD SA A ?

9. The most important communication responsibility of supervisors is to provide accurate information to employees about job assignments.
    D SD SA A ?

10. The most important communication skill that a supervisor can have is the skill of effective listening.
    A SA SD D ?

Employee Discipline

11. Progressive discipline means administering a less severe penalty for an initial violation of a work rule and more severe penalties for repeat violations.

    A SA SD D ?

12. Supervisors should administer discipline at the site of a work rule violation immediately after the violation has occurred in a fair and decisive manner.

    D SD SA A ?

13. Discipline as a concept is punitive and should be used only as a last resort.

    D SD SA A ?

14. In order to preserve relationships with employees, discipline should usually be administered by the personnel department, not by the employee's supervisor.

    D SD SA A ?

15. Most employees want their supervisors to take disciplinary action with those who violate work rules.

    A SA SD D ?

Empowerment

16. In empowered work forces competent individuals independently make decisions and engage in primarily one-on-one communication with each other.

    D SD SA A ?

17. Empowered employees respond best to a directive leadership style.

    D SD SA A ?

18. The empowerment principle of shared responsibility applies equally to task performance and to the sharing of rewards.

    A SA SD D ?

19. Facilitative leadership is more suitable for team building purposes than it is for developing an empowered work force.

    D SD SA A ?

20. In an empowered work force the primary responsibility for offering guidance and performance coaching is transferred to the employees.

    D SD SA A ?

Human Relations

21. Human relations practices usually have a greater direct impact on morale and job satisfaction than they do on labor productivity.

    A SA SD D ?

22. Leaders can improve their human relations practices by treating employees like they would want to be treated in similar situations.

    A SA SD D ?

23.	Human relations deals with how employees are treated rather than with how their skills are used.	A SA SD D ?
24.	The most successful human relations practices are those based on the friendships and personal relationships that supervisors often develop with employees.	D SD SA A ?
25.	In order to maintain harmony, supervisors should always match work assignments with the interests, personality and preferences of employees.	D SD SA A ?

Leadership

26.	A disadvantage of leading through the power of expertise is that employees could develop dependencies on the leader that might stifle their creativity	A SA SD D ?
27.	In order to be effective a leader must sincerely like people.	D SD SA A ?
28.	The most effective leaders consistently use the same leadership style in all situations.	D SD SA A ?
29.	In general, a delegative leadership style is more effective than other leadership styles in obtaining the full commitment of employees to a task.	D SD SA A ?
30.	Leaders cannot lead unless followers willingly accept and follow their leadership.	A SA SD D ?

Motivation

31.	Positive reinforcement is a motivational technique based on a carefully controlled system of rewards for desired performance.	A SA SD D ?
32.	Motivation is based on a person's needs, not his or her goals.	D SD SA A ?
33.	Employees who perform routine, repetitive tasks are usually less productive than employees whose tasks are varied and challenging.	D SD SA A ?
34.	Employees will usually be motivated by the prospect of receiving an important reward even if the probability that they can attain the required level of performance is doubtful.	D SD SA A ?
35.	Because most supervisors have little control over organization policy there is not much that they can personally do to motivate the average worker.	D SD SA D ?

Performance Management

36. In order to be effective and meaningful, a performance appraisal interview should focus exclusively on the supervisor's evaluation of the employee's job performance.   **D SD SA A ?**

37. Supervisors should never discriminate among employees, even on the basis of employees' job performance.   **D SD SA A ?**

38. It is more important for employees to clearly understand what the standards are for a job than to know how well they performed the job.   **D SD SA A ?**

39. Satisfied employees who are paid more will almost always perform better than dissatisfied employees who are paid less.   **D SD SA A ?**

40. In general, quantitative job standards cannot properly be applied to non-production jobs like those performed by office and clerical employees.   **D SD SA A ?**

Planning and Organization

41. The planning function involves setting objectives and developing strategies by which the objectives can be accomplished.   **A SA SD D ?**

42. In order for an objective to be valid it must be one of the following: precise or measurable or realistic.   **D SD SA A ?**

43. Plans developed by higher level managers usually have about the same time spans as those developed by first level supervisors.   **D SD SA A ?**

44. An important part of the planning function is the process of actually gathering the resources necessary to implement a plan.   **D SD SA A ?**

45. PERT (Program Evaluation and Review Technique), CPM (Critical Path Method) and GANTT charts are used exclusively in the planning function.   **D SD SA A ?**

Problem Solving/Decision Making

46. The first step that should be followed when solving a problem is to develop practicable alternative solutions for the problem.   **D SD SA A ?**

47. Decision making and problem solving methods are essentially the same.   **A SA SD D ?**

48. The first step in the decision making process should be to accurately define the issue or problem.   **A SA SD D ?**

49. Creative problem solving is a systematic method that involves both structured and open-ended thinking.   **A SA SD D ?**

50. The first step of most problem solving methods is to gather facts.   **D SD SA A ?**

Quality and Continuous Improvement

51. Although most employees enjoy participating in quality improvement programs, their suggestions have relatively little impact on product or service quality.   **D SD SA A ?**

52. The primary responsibility for ensuring that a high quality product or service is produced should be assigned to an organization's quality assurance department.   **D SD SA A ?**

53. Quality improvement teams, cause-effect analysis and statistical techniques can only be used effectively in manufacturing or production operations.   **D SD SA A ?**

54. According to total quality management philosophy, the "customer" is defined as the end user of the organization's products or services.   **D SD SA A ?**

55. The main focus in total quality management is on the prompt detection of undesirable quality variances in the final product or service of an organization.   **D SD SA A ?**

Team Building

56. An effective team usually deals with constructive criticism by using group process techniques like explaining, justifying and defending.   **D SD SA A ?**

57. Synergism occurs when on a given task the performance of the team is better than the performance of the best individual on the team.   **A SA SD D ?**

58. Teamwork is a good practice but studies show that constructive competition usually results in greater productivity improvement.   **D SD SA A ?**

59. A major strategy for team building is to increase the awareness of team members about their own group processes.   **A SA SD D ?**

60. An effective work team views any form of conflict as undesirable.   **D SD SA A ?**

Time Management

61. Time management problems can usually be avoided by doing thing efficiently.

    D SD SA A ?

62. Delegation makes employees responsible for results rather than for activities.

    A SA SD D ?

63. A good way to save time is to look for short cuts in management functions.

    D SD SA A ?

64. Staying busy and active is the best way to get the most out of a day.

    D SD SA A ?

65. The "ABC" system is a method for prioritizing activities.

    A SA SD D ?

Training

66. There are no accurate methods that can be used to measure the affect of a training program on an employee's level of job performance.

    D SD SA A ?

67. In order to expedite on-the-job training for new employees, senior employees should show them all the short cuts to performing a job.

    D SD SA A ?

68. The term "conscious-incompetence" means that a person knows that he or she has knowledge and/or skill deficiencies in certain job tasks.

    A SA SD D ?

69. It is more difficult to modify a person's attitude or behavior than it is to increase his or her knowledge or skill.

    A SA SD D ?

70. The best method for training new employees is to carefully tell them how the job is to be performed.

    D SD SA A ?

Work Assignment

71. In order to avoid unnecessary conflict, supervisors should assign relatively unpleasant tasks mainly to those employees who are willing to perform them.

    D SD SA A ?

72. If two employees are equally qualified then their work assignments should always be based on their respective seniority.

    D SD SA A ?

73. The best time to discuss performance standards with an employee is during an appraisal interview rather than when work assignments are made.   **D SD SA A ?**

74. As a general rule, work assignments should always be made on the basis of seniority, qualifications, and personal interests -- in that order.   **D SD SA A ?**

75. The best way to determine if an employee understands a work assignment is to watch for "body language" signals like a nod of the head or a smile.   **D SD SA A ?**

APPENDIX

This appendix contains reproducible scoring
grids for the TNAT and an interpretation guide
for test respondents. Both the scoring grids
and interpretation guide should be given to
each test respondent during his/her feedback
session.

Training Needs
Assessment Test
Personal Test Profile

Date:
Name:
Organization:

The purpose of this guide is to enable you to interpret the results of the *Training Needs Assessment Test* (TNAT). The TNAT is designed to help identify strengths and development needs in skill areas that are important to anyone who has, or aspires to have, management, supervisory or other leadership responsibilities. The focus of the test and the profile is on career and professional development and on management, supervisory and leadership performance development.

The TNAT consists of 75 objective test items distributed among 15 skill dimensions. The TNAT profile presents composite scores for each measured skill and leadership style dimension. Results are shown as arithmetic means within a value range of 15.0 (**Low Training Need**) to 0.0 (**High Training Need**) for individual test items. The test results of individual respondents can be compared with the normative data in this guide which has been derived from field testing the TNAT among mixed male and female populations of first level supervisors and middle managers from both industrial and service organizations.

Definitions for the 15 management, supervisory and leadership skill dimensions measured by the TNAT are:

Coaching & Counseling: The supervisor's responsibility for coaching and counseling, coaching as a developmental process focusing on job performance, coaching to confront subordinates about performance issues, counseling employees about problems, complaints or grievances.

Communication: The supervisor's responsibility to communicate effectively, the nature and process of communication, communication channels, listening skills.

Employee Discipline: The purpose and objective of discipline, progressive discipline, the supervisor's responsibility to administer discipline, principles of administering discipline.

Empowerment: Empowerment concept and principles, shared responsibility, involvement and teamwork, facilitative leadership.

Human Relations: The concept of human relations, human relations supervisory techniques, the effects of human relations practices on morale and productivity, fairness, consistency and uniformity.

Leadership: The basic concept of leadership, leadership as a power of influence, leadership styles and characteristics, situational leadership.

Motivation: The supervisor's responsibility to motivate employees, the nature of motivation, how motivation works, understanding the affects of motivation on job performance.

Performance Management: Setting and communicating job standards, evaluative and developmental performance counseling, performance appraisal, understanding job satisfaction in relation to job performance.

Planning & Organizing: Anticipating future events, setting precise, measurable and realistic objectives, developing plans and strategies to accomplish objectives, identifying and gathering the resources necessary to put plans into action.

Problem Solving/Decision Making: Problem solving versus decision making, problem solving and decision making steps, creative problem solving.

Quality & Continuous Improvement: Fully meeting customers' needs and expectations, prevention versus detection, responsibility for quality work, employee participation in continuous improvement.

Team Building: Team interaction and group process, team effectiveness and conflict, synergistic team work, team work and competition.

Time Management: The basic concept of time management, eliminating time wasters, time management principles, delegation.

Training: Principles of learning, effective vs. ineffective training methods, measurement of training results.

Work Assignments: Work assignments and performance standards, fair versus unfair work assignments, the basis for making work assignments, ensuring employees understand work assignments.

Interpreting Your Test Results

A Personal Test Profile containing your TNAT results will be given to you by your test facilitator. Training and development needs for the titled skill dimensions (Coaching & Counseling, Communication, etc.) are suggested whenever your score falls below the norm for each skill dimension (see norm scale below). However, in some cases the norm itself is relatively low, i.e. 6.6 against a 15.0 maximum. This simply means that many employees who have taken the TNAT need development in those areas. Because of this we strongly suggest that you would benefit from training and development whenever your score falls below a mean of 10.0, even if the norm is lower. The TNAT is designed so that there is an appropriate "universe of content" for each skill dimension. Therefore, if a training need is indicated for a particular skill dimension the full subject area, not just certain individual subject items, should be the focus of training and development. It should be noted that the TNAT measures **knowledge** and **beliefs** about various management concepts and principles --- not necessarily management behavior. However, research has strongly indicated that the actual work behavior of most employees is congruent with their knowledge and beliefs about the subject.

You should keep in mind that this test has been designed for developmental purposes. Low scores do not necessarily indicate low on-the-job work performance or lack of suitability for a job position. Rather, they may suggest that your performance can be optimized if you receive further development in the identified areas. Also, the test is not designed to be used as an employment or promotion selection instrument.

Normative Data in Arithmetic Means

Dimension	Norm	Dimension	Norm	Dimension	Norm
Coaching & Counseling	8.4	Leadership	6.6	Quality/Cont. Impv.	6.9
Communication	9.9	Motivation	7.2	Team Building	10.5
Employee Discipline	9.6	Performance Mgt.	7.2	Time Management	7.2
Empowerment	6.9	Planning & Organizing	6.9	Training	10.8
Human Relations	8.7	Problem Sol./Dec. Mkng	5.7	Work Assignments	9.9

TNAT SCORING FORMAT AND PERSONAL TEST PROFILE FOR: _____

COACHING & COUNSELING

Item No.	(a)	(b)	(c)	(d)	(e)	
1	A	SA	SD	D	?	S
2	D	SD	SA	A	?	E
3	A	SA	SD	D	?	T
4	D	SD	SA	A	?	S
5	D	SD	SA	A	?	C
	x3	x2	x1	x0	x0	O
	+	+	+	+ 0	+ 0 =	R
						E

COMMUNICATION

Item No.	(a)	(b)	(c)	(d)	(e)	
6	A	SA	SD	D	?	S
7	D	SD	SA	A	?	E
8	D	SD	SA	A	?	T
9	D	SD	SA	A	?	S
10	A	SA	SD	D	?	C
	x3	x2	x1	x0	x0	O
	+	+	+	+ 0	+ 0 =	R
						E

EMPLOYEE DISCIPLINE

Item No.	(a)	(b)	(c)	(d)	(e)	
11	A	SA	SD	D	?	S
12	D	SD	SA	A	?	E
13	D	SD	SA	A	?	T
14	D	SD	SA	A	?	S
15	A	SA	SD	D	?	C
	x3	x2	x1	x0	x0	O
	+	+	+	+ 0	+ 0 =	R
						E

EMPOWERMENT

Item No.	(a)	(b)	(c)	(d)	(e)	
16	D	SD	SA	A	?	S
17	D	SD	SA	A	?	E
18	A	SA	SD	D	?	T
19	D	SD	SA	A	?	S
20	D	SD	SA	A	?	C
	x3	x2	x1	x0	x0	O
	+	+	+	+ 0	+ 0 =	R
						E

HUMAN RELATIONS

Item No.	(a)	(b)	(c)	(d)	(e)	
21	A	SA	SD	D	?	S
22	A	SA	SD	D	?	E
23	A	SA	SD	D	?	T
24	D	SD	SA	A	?	S
25	D	SD	SA	A	?	C
	x3	x2	x1	x0	x0	O
	+	+	+	+ 0	+ 0 =	R
						E

LEADERSHIP

Item No.	(a)	(b)	(c)	(d)	(e)	
26	A	SA	SD	D	?	S
27	D	SD	SA	A	?	E
28	D	SD	SA	A	?	T
29	D	SD	SA	A	?	S
30	A	SA	SD	D	?	C
	x3	x2	x1	x0	x0	O
	+	+	+	+ 0	+ 0 =	R
						E

TNAT SCORING FORMAT AND PERSONAL TEST PROFILE FOR:

MOTIVATION

Item No.	RESPONSES (a)	(b)	(c)	(d)	(e)	SET SCORE
31	A	SA	SD	D	?	
32	D	SD	SA	A	?	
33	D	SD	SA	A	?	
34	D	SD	SA	A	?	
35	D	SD	SA	A	?	
	x3	x2	x1	x0	x0	
	+ __	+ __	+ __	+ 0	+ 0	=

PERFORMANCE MANAGEMENT

Item No.	RESPONSES (a)	(b)	(c)	(d)	(e)	SET SCORE
36	D	SD	SA	A	?	
37	D	SD	SA	A	?	
38	D	SD	SA	A	?	
39	D	SD	SA	A	?	
40	D	SD	SA	A	?	
	x3	x2	x1	x0	x0	
	+ __	+ __	+ __	+ 0	+ 0	=

PLANNING AND ORGANIZATION

Item No.	RESPONSES (a)	(b)	(c)	(d)	(e)	SET SCORE
41	A	SA	SD	D	?	
42	D	SD	SA	A	?	
43	D	SD	SA	A	?	
44	D	SD	SA	A	?	
45	D	SD	SA	A	?	
	x3	x2	x1	x0	x0	
	+ __	+ __	+ __	+ 0	+ 0	=

PROBLEM SOLVING/DECISION MAKING:

Item No.	RESPONSES (a)	(b)	(c)	(d)	(e)	SET SCORE
46	D	SD	SA	A	?	
47	A	SA	SD	D	?	
48	A	SA	SD	D	?	
49	A	SA	SD	D	?	
50	D	SD	SA	A	?	
	x3	x2	x1	x0	x0	
	+ __	+ __	+ __	+ 0	+ 0	=

QUALITY & CONTINUOUS IMPROVEMENT

Item No.	RESPONSES (a)	(b)	(c)	(d)	(e)	SET SCORE
51	D	SD	SA	A	?	
52	D	SD	SA	A	?	
53	D	SD	SA	A	?	
54	D	SD	SA	A	?	
55	D	SD	SA	A	?	
	x3	x2	x1	x0	x0	
	+ __	+ __	+ __	+ 0	+ 0	=

TEAM BUILDING

Item No.	RESPONSES (a)	(b)	(c)	(d)	(e)	SET SCORE
56	D	SD	SA	A	?	
57	A	SA	SD	D	?	
58	D	SD	SA	A	?	
59	A	SA	SD	D	?	
60	D	SD	SA	A	?	
	x3	x2	x1	x0	x0	
	+ __	+ __	+ __	+ 0	+ 0	=

TNAT SCORING FORMAT AND PERSONAL TEST PROFILE FOR:

TIME MANAGEMENT

Item No.	(a)	(b)	RESPONSES (c)	(d)	(e)	SET SCORE
61	D	SD	SA	A	?	
62	A	SA	SD	D	?	
63	D	SD	SA	A	?	
64	D	SD	SA	A	?	
65	A	SA	SD	D	?	
	x3	x2	x1	x0	x0	
	+	+	+	0	+ 0 =	

TRAINING

Item No.	(a)	(b)	RESPONSES (c)	(d)	(e)	SET SCORE
66	D	SD	SA	A	?	
67	D	SD	SA	A	?	
68	A	SA	SD	D	?	
69	A	SA	SD	D	?	
70	D	SD	SA	A	?	
	x3	x2	x1	x0	x0	
	+	+	+	0	+ 0 =	

WORK ASSIGNMENT

Item No.	(a)	(b)	RESPONSES (c)	(d)	(e)	SET SCORE
71	D	SD	SA	A	?	
72	D	SD	SA	A	?	
73	D	SD	SA	A	?	
74	D	SD	SA	A	?	
75	D	SD	SA	A	?	
	x3	x2	x1	x0	x0	
	+	+	+	0	+ 0 =	

COMPOSITE SCORE GRID

MEASUREMENT DIMENSIONS	HIGH 1	2	3	4	5	TRAINING NEED SET SCORES 6	7	8	9	10	11	12	13	14	LOW 15
COACHING AND COUNSELING															
COMMUNICATION															
EMPLOYEE DISCIPLINE															
EMPOWERMENT															
HUMAN RELATIONS															
LEADERSHIP															
MOTIVATION															
PERFORMANCE MANAGEMENT															
PLANNING AND ORGANIZATION															
PROBLEM SOLVING/DECISION MAKING															
QUALITY & CONTINUOUS IMPROVEMENT															
TEAM BUILDING															
TIME MANAGEMENT															
TRAINING															
WORK ASSIGNMENT															

Participant Booklet for

TRAINING NEEDS ASSESSMENT TEST

by Louis E. Tagliaferri, Ph.D.

MD-129

DATE: _____

CODE (N): _____ CODE (O): _____

NAME: _____

ORGANIZATION: _____

Instructions: Inside are 75 statements about work related conditions, practices or situations. Consider each of these from the perspective of someone who holds a leadership role in a typical business, industrial or governmental organization. Decide the extent to which you agree or disagree with each statement. Then circle the letter(s) or symbol to the right of each statement that best corresponds with your opinion. **A=Agree, SA=Somewhat Agree, SD=Somewhat Disagree, D=Disagree and ?= Uncertain**

Test Items	Response Scale
01. Coaching involves confronting employees about job performance problems.	A SA SD D ?
02. It is more appropriate for an employee to be counseled about a job related problem by an organization's personnel or human resources department than by the employee's supervisor.	A SA SD D ?
03. The best way for a supervisor to handle an emotional complaint by an employee is to first listen carefully and allow the employee to "blow off steam."	A SA SD D ?
04. A sign of a smoothly running work unit is the absence of complaints.	A SA SD D ?
05. Coaching, counseling and mentoring are interchangeable terms that describe the same managerial function.	A SA SD D ?
06. The communication process is not complete until the message receiver acknowledges receipt and understanding of the message.	A SA SD D ?
07. Department meetings, policy manuals, the "grapevine," and bulletin board notices are all examples of formal communication channels.	A SA SD D ?
08. The most effective form of communication is a graphic illustration that is supplemented by a written explanation of the illustration.	A SA SD D ?
09. The most important communication responsibility of supervisors is to provide accurate information to employees about job assignments.	A SA SD D ?
10. The most important communication skill that a supervisor can have is the skill of effective listening.	A SA SD D ?
11. Progressive discipline means administering a less severe penalty for an initial violation of a work rule and more severe penalties for repeat violations.	A SA SD D ?
12. Supervisors should administer discipline at the site of a work rule violation immediately after the violation has occurred in a fair and decisive manner.	A SA SD D ?
13. Discipline as a concept is a punitive and should only be used as a last resort.	A SA SD D ?
14. In order to preserve relationships with employees, discipline should usually be administered by the personnel department, not by the employee's supervisor.	A SA SD D ?
15. Most employees want their supervisors to take disciplinary action with those who violate work rules.	A SA SD D ?

Test Items	Response Scale
16. In empowered work forces competent individuals independently make decisions and engage in primarily one-on-one communication with each other.	A SA SD D ?
17. Empowered employees respond best to a directive leadership style.	A SA SD D ?
18. The empowerment principle of shared responsibility applies equally to task performance and to the sharing of rewards.	A SA SD D ?
19. Facilitative leadership is more suitable for team building purposes than it is for developing an empowered work force.	A SA SD D ?
20. In an empowered work force the primary responsibility for offering guidance and performance coaching is transferred to the employees.	A SA SD D ?
21. Human relations practices usually have a greater direct impact on morale and job satisfaction than they do on labor productivity.	A SA SD D ?
22. Leaders can improve their human relations practices by treating employees like they would want to be treated in similar situations.	A SA SD D ?
23. Human relations deals with how employees are treated rather than with how their skills are used.	A SA SD D ?
24. The most successful human relations practices are those based on the friendships and personal relationships that supervisors often develop with employees.	A SA SD D ?
25. In order to maintain harmony, supervisors should always match work assignments with the interests, personality and preferences of employees.	A SA SD D ?
26. A disadvantage of leading through the power of expertise is that employees could develop dependencies on the leader that might stifle their creativity.	A SA SD D ?
27. In order to be effective a leader must sincerely like people.	A SA SD D ?
28. The most effective leaders consistently use the same leadership style in all situations.	A SA SD D ?
29. In general, a delegative leadership style is more effective than other leadership styles in obtaining the full commitment of employees to a task.	A SA SD D ?
30. Leaders cannot lead unless followers willingly accept and follow their leadership.	A SA SD D ?

Test Items	Response Scale	Test Items	Response Scale

31. Positive reinforcement is a motivational technique based on a carefully controlled system of rewards for desired performance. A SA SD D ?

32. Motivation is based on a person's needs, not his or her goals. A SA SD D ?

33. Employees who perform routine, repetitive tasks are usually less productive than employees whose tasks are varied and challenging. A SA SD D ?

34. Employees will usually be motivated by the prospect of receiving an important reward even if the probability that they can attain the required level of performance is doubtful. A SA SD D ?

35. Because most supervisors have little control over organizational policy there is not much that they can do personally to motivate the average employee. A SA SD D ?

36. In order to be effective and meaningful, a performance appraisal interview should focus exclusively on the supervisor's evaluation of the employee's job performance. A SA SD D ?

37. Supervisor's should never discriminate among employees, even on the basis of an employee's job performance. A SA SD D ?

38. It is more important for employees to clearly understand what the standards are for a job than to know how well they performed the job. A SA SD D ?

39. Satisfied employees who are paid more will almost always perform better than dissatisfied employees who are paid less. A SA SD D ?

40. In general, quantitative job standards cannot properly be applied to non-production jobs like those performed by office and clerical employees. A SA SD D ?

41. The planning function involves setting objectives and developing strategies by which the objectives can be accomplished. A SA SD D ?

42. In order for an objective to be valid it must be one of the following: precise or measurable or realistic. A SA SD D ?

43. Plans developed by higher level managers usually have about the same time spans as those developed by first level supervisors. A SA SD D ?

44. An important part of the planning function is the process of actually gathering the resources necessary to implement a plan. A SA SD D ?

45. PERT (Program Evaluation and Review Technique), CPM (Critical Path Method) and GANTT charts are used exclusively in the planning function. A SA SD D ?

46. The first step that should be followed when solving a problem is to develop practicable alternative solutions for the problem. A SA SD D ?

47. Decision making and problem solving methods are essentially the same. A SA SD D ?

48. The first step in the decision making process should be to accurately define the issue or problem. A SA SD D ?

49. Creative problem solving is a systematic method that involves both structured and open-ended thinking. A SA SD D ?

50. The first step of most problem solving methods is to gather facts. A SA SD D ?

51. Although most employees enjoy participating in quality improvement programs, their suggestions have relatively little impact on product or service quality. A SA SD D ?

52. The primary responsibility for ensuring that a high quality product or service is produced should be assigned to an organization's quality assurance department. A SA SD D ?

53. Quality improvement teams, cause-effect analysis and statistical techniques can only be used effectively in manufacturing or production operations. A SA SD D ?

54. According to total quality management philosophy, the "customer" is defined as the end user of the organization's products or services. A SA SD D ?

55. The main focus in total quality management is on the prompt detection of undesirable quality variances in the final product or service of an organization. A SA SD D ?

56. An effective team usually deals with constructive criticism by using group process techniques like explaining, justifying and defending. A SA SD D ?

57. Synergism occurs when on a given task the performance of the team is better than the performance of the best individual on the team. A SA SD D ?

Test Items	Response Scale	Test Items	Response Scale

Test Items

58. Teamwork is a good practice but studies show that constructive competition usually results in greater productivity improvement.

A SA SD D ?

59. A major strategy for team building is to increase the awareness of team members about their own group processes.

A SA SD D ?

60. An effective work team views any form of conflict as undesirable.

A SA SD D ?

61. Time management problems can usually be avoided by doing things efficiently.

A SA SD D ?

62. Delegation makes employees responsible for results rather than for activities.

A SA SD D ?

63. A good way to save time is to look for short cuts in management functions.

A SA SD D ?

64. Staying busy and active is the best way to get the most out of a day.

A SA SD D ?

65. The "ABC" system is a method for prioritizing activities.

A SA SD D ?

66. There are no accurate methods that can be used to measure the affect of a training program on an employee's level of job performance.

A SA SD D ?

67. In order to expedite on-the-job training for new employees, senior employees should show them all the short cuts to performing a job.

A SA SD D ?

Test Items

68. The term "conscious-incompetence" means that a person knows that he or she has knowledge and/or skills deficiencies in certain job tasks.

A SA SD D ?

69. It is more difficult to modify a person's attitude or behavior than it is to increase his or her knowledge or skill.

A SA SD D ?

70. The best method for training new employees is to carefully tell them how the job is to be performed.

A SA SD D ?

71. In order to avoid unnecessary conflict, supervisors should assign relatively unpleasant tasks mainly to those employees who are willing to perform them.

A SA SD D ?

72. If two employees are equally qualified then their work assignments should always be based on their respective seniority.

A SA SD D ?

73. The best time to discuss performance standards with an employee is during an appraisal interview rather than when work assignments are made.

A SA SD D ?

74. As a general rule, work assignments should always be made on the basis of seniority, qualifications, and personal interests – in that order.

A SA SD D ?

75. The best way to determine if an employee understands a work assignment is to watch for "body language" signals like a nod of the head or a smile.

A SA SD D ?

How to Use it

The Intercultural Communication Inventory (ICI) is most effective when used as a training aid to increase knowledge and awareness about intercultural communication concepts and principles. It can serve equally well as an excellent "ice breaker" or as a closure exercise. Although designed primarily as a learning instrument, the ICI can also be used to help evaluate the effectiveness of a diversity or intercultural relations workshop or seminar by being administered as a "post-test." Still another use is to help stimulate intercultural communication discussion among continuous improvement teams, self-directed work teams and other work unit teams.

In order to obtain optimum value from the ICI, facilitators should first read both this guide and the instrument in its entirety. Facilitators should have (or acquire) a fundamental understanding about diversity management and intercultural communication before they use the ICI or conduct an intercultural communication training session. Many good references are readily available if it is necessary to review the subject further.

One copy of the Respondent Booklet is required for each person in the class, team or workshop. Distribute the booklets to all participants. Explain your purpose for administering the instrument and then read the instructions aloud. Allow about 15 minutes for completion. When all participants are finished, ask them to refer to their copy of the inventory. Provide them with the correct answer and conduct a brief discussion about each point covered. Use the intercultural communication tips in the following section of this guide and/or other supplemental material as the basis for this discussion.

Answers & Intercultural Communication Tips

01. True. Women, minorities and people from other countries who come from different cultural backgrounds are the most rapidly growing sector of the work force.

02. True. This is "cultural shock." Cultural shock is an intercultural dysfunction that can affect people of all cultures. It also can cause serious identity problems.

03. False. In fact, this is one of the major reasons why communication between and among people of different cultures often becomes distorted. Misunderstandings occur when people of one culture, including racial, ethnic and religious minorities, interpret the verbal and non-verbal behavior of people of other cultures on the basis of their own values, customs and codes.

04. False. There is often very little correlation between a person's accent and their comprehension and ease of use of the English language.

05. False. Human needs and traits may be the same or similar but there are often many significant differences in gestures and expressions. The ringed fingers "OK" symbol, for example, means that everything is "OK" in some cultures but is an obscene gesture in others.

06. False. A good example can be found by studying ancient cultures like the Mayan. Although having a low level of technology as we know it today, the Mayan culture was very advanced and sophisticated in other ways.

07. False. Some cultures place such heavy emphasis on group and team behavior that individuals would be embarrassed if their personal achievements were singled out.

08. True. Although sometimes misleading, first impressions often provide valuable information about a person's profession, economic status, age, personality and other characteristics.

09. True. Further, most people unconsciously become quite proficient at reading the body language of others. The problem is that body language communication is not identical among all cultures.

10. False. The North American communication culture is low context. High context cultures rely heavily on the implied meaning of what is said or not said and how it is said. North Americans are much more explicit and direct.

11. True. See #8 above.

12. True. This can cause the misunderstanding that employees of these cultures do not take the initiative or that they are not motivated.

13. True. Space or distance between speakers has meaning and varies between cultures. In some cultures, it is common for relative strangers to speak in literally face-to-face closeness while, in other cultures, this would be considered too intimate.

14. False. Just the opposite is true; they vary considerably among the cultures of the world.

15. False. In some cultures, smiling and nodding are ways to cover up embarrassment or attempts to please the speaker.

16. False. Many of the world's cultures see time as being much more elastic than the way North Americans see it. For example, the North American focus on adhering to schedules and deadlines is not shared the same way by people in Arab and Latin American countries.

17. True. A common misunderstanding is that it is non-verbal communication.

18. False. All of these factors affect not only interpersonal relationships but also communication. In fact, if not properly understood by communicators they can seriously distort communication between cultures.

19. False. What is most important is for managers and employees of different cultures to develop a better understanding of their respective cultural differences and how these differences can affect relationships and communication.

20. False. Foreign language skills can help. However, cultural awareness and effective intercultural communication, even through interpreters if necessary, is more important.

21. True. Equal Employment Opportunity and Affirmative Action, though both very important, are equity issues. It is possible to have EEO and Affirmative Action programs and still not effectively manage diversity or have effective intercultural communication.

22. False. This may be appropriate when communicating with other low context cultures. However, many cultures within the work place are high context cultures which require less direct, holistic communication.

23. True. Ethnocentrism occurs when cultural groups increasingly focus on their own culture. Communication difficulties increase when two or more ethnocentric groups attempt to communicate with each other. Not sharing common values, etc., they often view the other person as a "stranger" and approach him/her with anxiety and uncertainty.

24. False. Very often they are unaware of the cultural differences and cannot understand why their communication is misinterpreted.

25. True. See #24 above.

Recommended Reading

Cherry, C., World Communication: Threat or Promise? New York, John Wiley & Sons, Inc., 1978.

Harris, Philip R. and Moran, Robert T., Managing Cultural Differences (2nd ed), Houston, Gulf Publishing Company, 1987.

Kim, Young Yun and Gudykunst, William B., Theories in Intercultural Communication, Newbury Park, CA, Sage Publications, 1988.

Samovar, Larry A. and Porter, Richard E., eds., Intercultural Communication: A Reader, Belmont, CA, Wadsworth Publishing, 1972.

Zimpfer, Forest and Underwood, Robert, The Status of International Business Communication Training in the 100 Largest Multinational United States Corporations, Ypsilanti, MI, Eastern Michigan University Report, 1989.

www.ingramcontent.com/pod-product-compliance
Lightning Source LLC
Chambersburg PA
CBHW080242180526
45167CB00006B/2378